I0037767

Thriving Leaders

THRIVING LEADERS

Learn the Skills to Lead Confidently

CLAIRE GRAY

Copyright © Claire Gray

All models copyright © Claire Gray

First published in 2022 | Melbourne

ISBN: 978-0-6456247-0-0 (pbk) eISBN: 978-0-6456247-1-7 (ebook)

A catalogue record for this book is available from the National Library of Australia

Edited by Joanna Yardley at The Editing House

Typeset, printed and bound in Australia by BookPOD

All rights reserved. No part of this publication may be reproduced by any means without the prior written consent of the publisher.

This book uses case studies to enforce the meaning behind its relevant chapter. Names have been omitted or changed to protect individual privacy where requested.

Every effort has been made to trace (and seek permission for use of) the original source of material used within this book. Where the attempt has been unsuccessful, the publisher would be pleased to hear from the author/publisher to rectify any omission.

This book is dedicated to my dad—I miss you.

Acknowledgements

It takes a village to write a book.

A massive heartfelt thanks to my family. Ben, my husband, has been an incredible support to me in life, love and parenting. I couldn't do it without you. Thank you for reading the first version of my manuscript and providing invaluable feedback. To my beautiful boys, Jackson and Harvey, I love you and you make me laugh every day.

I'd like to thank the fabulous leaders who allowed me to interview them and share their leadership success: Tony Davies, Sandy Morrow, Jimmy Stewart and Will Brook.

Thanks to Liz Compton, Jon Eddy, Steve McEwin, Kate Whitehill, John Cox, Drago Mitkov, James Whitehill and Sarah White for letting me share your stories.

I'd like to thank Jon Eddy, James Whitehill, Anika Patel and Zoe Noble for reading parts of the book, providing feedback and being a sense check. Your support helped me to work through my thinking and it was reassuring.

To the very talented editor Joanna Yardley, who worked her magic and made my ideas sound even better.

To my friend and talented graphic designer Lara Evans for designing my book cover (which I love), my logo and the Thriving Leaders Model.

To Josephine Marie Lumanog and Emma Fletcher for designing the models within the book and for being a part of the Thriving Culture team (present and past).

Thank you to Sylvie Blair from BookPOD for publishing the book.

Thank you to Anita Saunders for your speedy proofreading.

Thank you Sam Mathers from the Candid Files for my mug shot.

Thanks to my wonderful clients who provided me with the experiences that have informed the book. To the participants who have attended my programs, teams and individuals I've coached, and those who have shared their wisdom—I've learnt so much from you all.

And finally, to my mum, just because I love you.

About Claire

Claire Gray is passionate about building high-performing teams and people so they can thrive.

She has worked with small businesses and large corporates across industries including Financial Services, Professional Services, Transport, Government, Mining, FMCG, Education and NFP in Australia and in the UK. Her many roles have been in People & Culture, Leadership, Organisational Design and Change Management.

Claire launched her own practice, Thriving Culture, in November 2018. She is an experienced Facilitator, Trainer, Speaker and Coach. Her strengths lie in understanding dynamics and asking powerful questions, and she is known for her enthusiasm and zestful nature. Claire enjoys helping individuals realise their potential and assists them in developing new and relevant skills so they can be effective at work and in life. She loves developing leadership capability, building high-performing teams and thriving cultures.

Claire has a number of qualifications and experiences:

- Master of Business (Human Resource Management).
- Bachelor of Behavioural Science.
- Professional Certified Coach with the International Coaching Federation.

- Certificate of Organisational Coaching with the Institute of Executive Coaching & Leadership.
- Team Coaching – Complex Adaptive Systems with the Global Team Coaching Institute.
- Certified Facet5 Practitioner (personality assessment).

As a daughter of two schoolteachers, Daryl and Pauline, learning and growth were important from a young age. Claire grew up in Melbourne, Australia, and now lives in Byron Bay with her husband, Ben, and two sons, Jackson and Harvey. She enjoys time at the beach, travelling and having a laugh with friends.

Claire runs highly successful leadership development programs and thriving teams sessions. And she coaches and speaks at events. For more information, please check out her website www.thrivingculture.com.au.

Contents

PART 1
UNDERSTAND SELF AND OTHERS

PART 2
EMPOWER AND DEVELOP YOUR TEAM

PART 3
CONNECT TO PURPOSE

Introduction

'I never lose. I either win or learn.'
—Nelson Mandela

Why I wrote this book

Recently, I started playing tennis again. I played when I was growing up and even participated in weekend competitions. But since my teenage years, I hadn't played and over time I lost my confidence. One day, after watching the Australian Open, I was inspired to pick up my racquet. After playing a bit of social tennis, I realised I needed some one-on-one coaching. Once I started, I was amazed at how quickly I progressed. For example, my forehand improved immediately after my coach corrected my grip and changed my stance. I also received feedback on my serve— my ball toss was too high. For me, this experience emphasised the power of practice, coaching and effective feedback loops. They are all critical to successfully developing a new skill. Leadership is no different.

This book brings together many leadership and high-performing team theories and my own extensive experience working with leaders to bring out their best. Most importantly, this book is actionable, which means you can practise and implement the techniques in your daily life.

Often, leaders with solid experience and technical capabilities are promoted into leadership positions. They find themselves leading a team and facing a variety of situations never previously encountered. If this is you, you know it can be challenging—especially when you don't have the essential tools. The result is often a loss of confidence.

This is why I decided to write this book. Time and time again, leaders come to me with a lack of confidence in their leadership abilities. I want to help change this for as many people as possible. To do this, I have compiled the leadership content, frameworks, practical tools and theory that I use every day in my Thriving Leaders Program.

By the end of this book, you will have the skills you need to lead confidently. You will learn how to bring out these skills in others so you can create high-performing, cohesive and engaged teams.

Who is this book for?

- Are you a leader who has never consciously studied or had leadership training?
- Have you recently been appointed to a leadership role?
- Have you been in your current role for a while?
- Are you a business owner?
- Are you simply aspiring to move into a leadership role?

Over the many years I have been training, coaching and facilitating, I have observed that leaders are promoted into their roles based on their technical capability and not their leadership experience. They are essentially put in a position of sink or swim.

Many organisations can't or don't invest in developing their people skills.

Leaders in these situations will continue to invest in their technical skills to stay current. This is important; however, what is equally, if not more, significant is investing in leadership development.

The research further supports this. When do you think most managers commence their leadership training? Intuitively, you would presume it to be early in their leadership careers.

On average, leaders move into their first position between the ages of 30–35 but they don't complete leadership training, on average, until 40–45—that's ten years after they started in their leadership positions (Zenger, 2012).

These leaders are left to observe what others have done and try to emulate their leadership. If they are lucky, they have a strong leader who can support them. Once they have completed leadership training, they must relearn new ways of leading and unlearn habits that have not been serving them.

This book is for leaders in this position. It will help speed up this process so you can understand what leadership can look like for you.

> 'Intelligence is traditionally viewed as the ability
> to think and learn. Yet in a turbulent world,
> there's another set of cognitive skills that might
> matter more: the ability to rethink and unlearn.'
> —Adam M. Grant

In my work as a leadership facilitator, coach and trainer, I continue to listen to the frustrations of leaders. Surprisingly, these frustrations are similar whether they are felt by first-time leaders or CEOs. These frustrations, which may also impact you, include:

- Not knowing how to manage different personality styles, especially those different to your own.
- Lacking confidence in how to have difficult conversations and avoiding issues that need to be dealt with.
- Not holding team members accountable, which leads to team members not having clarity of expectations.
- Delegated work doesn't meet your standards, which results in you doing more than you should and subsequently feeling stressed and exhausted.
- Feeling like you are not good enough to be in the role (enter imposter syndrome), which impacts your confidence and holds you back (enter stage left limiting belief).
- Going from teammate to manager where it is difficult to gain authority and respect from your team.
- Managing everyone the same way—thinking that one size fits all.
- Being told to be more or less assertive or to be more or less empathetic.
- Dealing with 'people' issues all the time, especially relationship issues between team members.
- Having the confidence to make the right decisions.
- Not feeling like you have the time to develop your people.
- Being so busy that you are reactive and short-sighted rather than taking time to focus on long-term strategy.

- Backing people into roles with increased responsibility and expectations and then finding they buckle under the pressure. Their ambition doesn't always match the reality as they don't deliver to the new expectation level.
- Trying to influence up and not always being heard.

I wanted to make this book as relevant and true to life as possible. As a result, the stories you will read are either personal experiences or real-life situations from clients with whom I have worked. Of course, some of the names and organisations have been adapted or omitted to allow anonymity.

Thriving Leaders Model

There are huge expectations placed upon leaders. Plus, there are many skills required to be successful. No one style or method is best; it is about developing your own style and adapting it to each situation.

I developed the Thriving Leaders Model after working with leaders who needed to develop skills in areas that were critical to their success. These particular areas are backed by theory and research. I've been using this model for years now and I have seen how effective it is in building leadership capability and high-performing teams.

The Thriving Leaders Model is broken into three parts:

- Understand self and others.
- Empower and develop team.
- Connect to purpose.

Within each part, you will develop two fundamental skills.

Understanding Self and Others

Here you will develop the skills to understand and articulate your authentic leadership style. We will explore how to build a high-performing team through purpose, relationships and accountability.

Empower and Develop Team

This is where you get practical on how to deliver and receive feedback and face difficult conversations. You will build skills to empower your team by taking a coaching approach. You will make the shift from telling your team what to do to asking powerful questions so they can solve their own problems.

Connect to Purpose

The final section explores the skills you need to hold your team accountable. You will learn to provide clarity and set goals. You will learn to better understand communication and how to influence your team through clear messaging.

The outcome of mastering these fundamental skills is a thriving and confident leader. Together, we will cover how to:

- Improve self-awareness and understand your natural leadership style.
- Build a high-performing team.
- Develop your team by effectively giving and receiving feedback.
- Empower team members by taking a coaching approach.
- Have the confidence to hold your team members accountable, and set expectations and goals.
- Communicate with impact through clear messaging.

Why read this book

This book will help you develop the skills and tools you need to lead your team confidently. Ultimately it will help you, your team and your organisation to thrive.

I understand that managers at all levels have significant daily responsibilities and that the immediate focus is usually the workload. Time is precious and often there is limited capacity to take on extra tasks. But what if this 'extra task' dramatically impacted your business performance, operations, productivity and professional relationships between employees? I'd argue that this isn't something 'extra', this is your role. By improving your productivity and performance as a thriving leader, you will get this time back as you will be operating more efficiently and empowering your team to grow and take on more challenges.

Leaders tend to focus on productivity gains through new tools and processes; however, much waste in organisations is due to poor leadership and conversations that were never had or were poorly handled. This investment in yourself will lead to a more productive organisation, more engaged employees and a more profitable business.

It is often difficult to measure the impact of leadership as it can be intangible. It has an indirect benefit and the flow-on business impacts cannot necessarily be isolated to leadership development alone. However, from my experience, I am confident it will improve employee engagement, which leads to a productive and motivated organisation, an increase in performance and a better bottom line.

I know some of you will be keen to understand the return on investment (ROI), so here are some facts and figures. Research from GBS Corporate Training (2017) states that productivity is decreased by 5–10% due to poor leadership, which can cost organisations millions each year. This is in addition to a 7% loss in annual sales. Better leadership can attribute to a 9–32% reduction in voluntary turnover. And according to a recent study, the cost to recruit has doubled to $23,860 per employee—proof that turnover is costly (Wightman, 2022).

DDI reports that one poor leader costs a company more than $126,000 annually due to low productivity, turnover and staff disengagement. People leave a boss, not a job. In fact, an industry trends study suggests seven out of ten employees quit their boss rather than their company (Williams, 2022).

We know that the more engaged an employee, the more productive and higher performing the organisation. Gallup reports that the single biggest reason that employees are not engaged is poor leadership.

It's time to step up and invest in your leadership skills. It's time to be the thriving leader you and your team needs.

How to use this book

When you first read this book, read it through a lens of curiosity. If you can, come with a beginner's mind like the Zen Buddhism concept of 'having an attitude of openness, eagerness, and lack of preconceptions when studying a subject'. Even if you are quite experienced, you will be more open to trying new things.

Each section lays out practical tools you can use and implement and there is a summary at the end of each chapter. There are activities and actions you can apply in your role—to bring what you have learnt to life. Some will read this book from cover to cover, while others may go directly to the chapter that is most relevant to what they need. This is up to you and will be based on what you want to get out of the book.

My mantra when writing this book was *done is better than perfect.* I share because 'taking action' is the mantra I'd like you to have when applying these skills in the workplace. This doesn't mean you need to change everything at once. You can start small, for example, preparing before that difficult conversation or asking more open questions. Even small incremental changes will amount to something significant in your leadership style. Of course, if you take no action, nothing will change.

When I read a book, I'm unimpressed when there is only one key message repeated in different ways. I promise that this is not that type of book. I'm too practical and your time is too valuable. So don't expect too much waffle. We will get to the point quickly and give you the tools you need to implement this behaviour change.

So for now, lean in and get ready to absorb some practical ways to improve your leadership— whether you are a first-time or long-time leader. I'm excited to be on this journey with you.

PART 1

Understand self and others

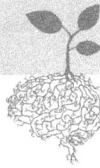

We've all had, or observed, leaders who have inspired our careers. Those leaders have a deep understanding of who they are, their values and strengths and what truly drives them.

But how often do *you* take time to think about how you want to lead? How will you be an intentional leader for your people every day? To do this, you must consider the impact of your own leadership style and how you can use that to bring out the best in your team. By truly understanding your strengths and natural style—and those of your team members—you can better understand and value your differences, which you can leverage to create a high-performing team.

In part 1, you will learn about your own leadership style so you can get the best out of yourself and your team. Then you will explore the elements of a high-performing team so you can create a thriving team culture.

CHAPTER 1

Leadership Style

*'To be aware of a single shortcoming
within oneself is more useful than to be
aware of a thousand in someone else.'*
—Dalai Lama

What is leadership?

Leadership is the act of inspiring and motivating a group of people towards a common goal and overcoming challenges to deliver results. Leadership is an action. Leadership is not a position, as anyone within an organisation can demonstrate leadership. Although this book focuses on people leadership, parts of this chapter are still relevant to self-leadership.

Leaders play a fundamental role in supporting people to learn and develop. Thriving leaders need to be able to build their team's effectiveness, face difficult conversations, provide direction, set goals, make decisions, manage change and communicate effectively.

I've been led by many great leaders over the years. And, like most, I've observed instances of poor leadership too. It is often through observing others that you determine the type of leader you want to be and the type of leader you don't.

Leadership is not one size fits all. You need to adapt your style to suit each situation. The more you understand yourself, the better you can understand others and lead them effectively. Leaders who want to be consistent yet don't adapt their style often get frustrated with the response from their team.

A leader needs to continue to develop and evolve on their leadership journey. They must be adaptable to today's ever-changing environments and have the skills and tools to lead and positively impact the business.

> *'Leadership is about making others better as a result of your presence and making sure that impact lasts in your absence.'*
> —Sheryl Sandberg

The expectations of a leader

Most literature focuses on the difference between leadership and management. The reality is, if you are leading a team, you will be doing both and more. Let's get clear on what those different expectations are of you as a leader.

Visionary: Inspire the team, set the vision, understand the strategic big picture and communicate this to your team. You are motivating your team for the future.

Manager: Direct your team, assign work, delegate, clarify expectations, give context about what needs to be delivered and followed up, and hold your team accountable.

Mentor: Impart your knowledge and wisdom and share stories of how you have approached situations in the past so that your team members can take what is relevant to them and apply it.

Coach: Ask powerful questions so the person you're coaching can come up with their own solution—one that is meaningful and useful for them.

Teacher: Train your team, impart and transfer knowledge and skills. This could mean showing them a new process or inducting them in the team so they can learn a new skill to be effective in their role.

Advisor: Share your specialist knowledge, give advice, problem solve together and offer solutions.

The final two components are often not in the job description but can take up considerable time.

Counsellor: Be a sounding board because people are human. We all go through difficult times in and outside of work and mental health issues are more prevalent than ever. This is the role of the listener. Use appropriate support like Employee Assistance Programs where applicable, as you are not a psychologist.

Mediator: Assist when two team members are having a disagreement and can't resolve it on their own.

As you can see, there is a huge expectation of you as a leader. Some days you may play all these roles, others just a few. The critical skill of a leader is reading the situation and determining what it is time for.

Leading through a natural disaster

In February 2022, the Northern Rivers region experienced the biggest flood in modern Australian history. I sat down with Tony Davies, CEO at Social Futures, to hear how he and his team led through the 2022 NSW floods.

Social Futures is a regional human services organisation that creates positive social change by working with communities to strengthen them and working with individuals so they can take control of their lives. The company's service delivery streams are in mental health, homelessness and disability. The organisation spans four offices and 120 of their 350 staff work in the heart of Lismore.

Here is Tony's account of the beginning of the 2022 NSW floods.

> *We had been through the floods five years earlier, in March 2017, which were considered at the time to be catastrophic. Fast forward to Sunday 27 February 2022, we were made aware of the weather warning for moderate to major flooding. Not knowing that the levee would overflow yet again, a team of people went in to prepare the offices—they moved everything from the ground floor to the first floor. We ensured our fleet of vehicles was on higher ground. We also checked in on staff who lived on the flood plain to see if they needed any help moving things. One staff member said she didn't need help as the floor level of her house was 12.7 metres above flood level. The community had pulled together, and everyone was very confident we had done all we could do.*

At 10 pm on Sunday night, I sent an email to the board advising them that our staff were safe, the fleet was on higher ground and the offices were prepared. And that although there would be water under houses with the flood level at 12.47 metres, this would be a 'dry run' of flood preparation for future flood events.

I was woken at 6 am to the phone ringing. It was the staff member who had their house at 12.7 metres to say that her daughter was standing on the table with water coming up her legs and that she didn't know whether they'd be saved because they couldn't get a boat. So obviously, the first concern went to the safety of our staff.

We quickly contacted staff who were at risk but had trouble getting through. We needed boats. I was expecting a very serious death toll. The water was more than 2 metres higher than in the previous flood. All four offices were destroyed.

We will discuss how Tony led Social Futures with different leadership styles during the NSW floods.

Leadership styles

Thriving leaders need to read a situation, understand its context and make a choice about the style of leadership that is appropriate.

There are many and varying types of leadership. In the book, *Head, Heart and Guts*, the authors discuss that whole leadership is required to be a successful leader—encompassing head (logic, analysing and processing), heart (emotional processing, values and relationships) and gut (intuition, courage and action). You need to set strategy with your head, empathise with your heart and take risks with your gut.

To be a successful 'authentic' leader, you need to balance being assertive, empathetic and adaptive. There can be tension between these three styles of leadership, for example, balancing being assertive and empathetic at the same time. The key word here is balance. You need to spin your authentic leadership dial to flex to the situation.

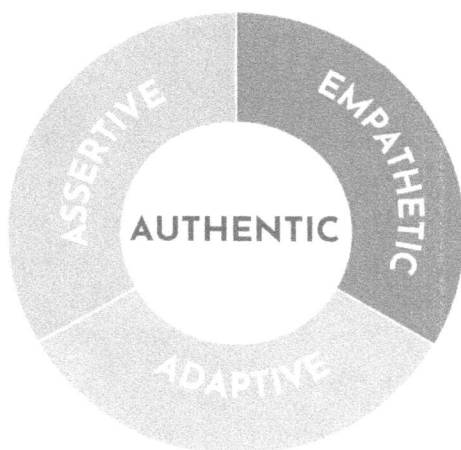

Authentic leadership

Authentic leadership is about being transparent, honest and genuine. According to Bill George in his book *Authentic Leadership*, 'Authentic leaders are driven by a moral and ethical purpose and never lose sight of their core values and principles. They lead with their hearts, cultivate long-term relationships, and demonstrate excellence through self-discipline'.

To be authentic leaders and wholeheartedly explore our true selves, we need to reflect on our strengths, values and purpose. This can feel uncomfortable and confusing to some and liberating and empowering to others. Taking the time to reflect on the type of leader you aspire to be means you can be more intentional in how you lead each day.

Authenticity is about purpose more than style. It is about dialling up or dialling down different parts of your personality based on the situation. There are many parts to our personalities and if we are in tune with what is happening around us, we can be what the situation requires. This takes emotional intelligence and the ability to understand ourselves and others. Consider it like the volume on the stereo: pump it up when a team member needs positive reinforcement and turn it down when a team member is upset and needs empathy. Alternatively, leave the dial in the middle when you need to give some constructive feedback that requires assertiveness balanced with compassion. This doesn't mean you need to be a chameleon and be all things to all people. Authentic leadership means discovering what types of leadership are required of you and applying them in a way that is genuine to you.

As Brené Brown says in the *Gifts of Imperfection,* 'Authenticity is a collection of choices that we have to make every day. It's about the choice to show up and be real. The choice to be honest. The choice to let our true selves be seen'. Adapting our style to meet our team members or the situation doesn't mean we are being inauthentic. The same approach for one team member potentially won't work for another. If you want to get the best out of your team, you need to be adaptable while also being true to yourself.

Authentic leadership takes courage. Showing your vulnerability further humanises you as a leader and shows others they can be vulnerable too. Vulnerability creates safety and trust, and staff feel more secure knowing you are genuine. It is okay to bring your true self to work. Authentically caring for your staff and getting to know them personally is a skill that sets leaders apart.

A Harvard Business Review article, *The Authenticity Paradox*, asks some key questions about authenticity. Can you be too authentic? Is it an excuse for staying in your comfort zone? Experiment with different leadership behaviours to see what works for you. Observe other leaders you admire, borrow and try out their behaviours to see if it feels right for you. Create the leadership narrative for the leader you want to be.

We are often told to be more professional at work. I was told this early on in my career. But the unintended consequence of this is we become more polished. We learn the corporate speak but we start becoming less of ourselves. We lose our sparkle. I have had to unlearn the corporate jargon and bring more of me into the work that I do, and it is something I am conscious of still.

How can you be a more authentic leader?

Assertive leadership

Assertive leadership requires a balance of good judgement, decision-making and being self-assured. Assertive leaders give team members certainty, especially in times of ambiguity. Assertive leaders communicate with confidence and conviction; they make people feel safe and secure.

Assertive leadership does not mean being aggressive, argumentative or opinionated. Assertive leaders still consult and get opinions and views from others. They are open to feedback from their team. They are quick to decide once this has occurred.

When leaders are not assertive, people feel uncertain. They are perceived as being indecisive, not holding strong views, and being overly agreeable and easily swayed. To build your assertive leadership muscle, you need to reflect on your decision-making process and how you communicate.

Tony shared how his assertive leadership came into play during the floods as fast, decisive decision-making was required for the safety of his staff and organisation.

After the floods, the senior management team came together quickly. The first priority was the safety and lives of our staff. You need to simplify your planning down to the core things that matter. At the point of crisis, you need to know what to do. Our priorities, in order of importance, were staff safety, secure our infrastructure and contribute to the community.

We created a flood management group that met daily. In the week following, we created working groups that helped with the clean-up in offices and staff members' houses. By the end of the week, we had teams of volunteers coming from everywhere. We had to act and make decisions quickly.

This extraordinary natural disaster and a global pandemic, all of which we thought were unthinkable, meant that more than ever, we needed to be persistent in our optimism. We followed the path we decided upon and stayed the course to provide

> certainty to our people. The only caveat was to not stick to the direction if the evidence clearly showed we needed to be adaptable. What I do now, far more than I used to, is stick to my guns and listen to people but be decisive.
>
> Tony provided certainty to his people. He created a simple plan and made decisions quickly.

Empathetic leadership

Empathy is the sincere ability to understand and share the feelings and needs of others. It means knowing what it's like to walk in their shoes and understand their point of view. Empathetic leaders can connect with many types of people. Having the ability to relate to others helps to build trusting relationships. Team members feel seen, heard and valued. Empathetic leaders may struggle with difficult conversations and providing constructive feedback, as they have a genuine concern for people's feelings.

Jacinda Ardern, the New Zealand Prime Minister, is the poster child of empathetic and compassionate leadership. She navigated a terrorist attack, a natural disaster and a pandemic in a short time—and all with a newborn in her arms. Her authenticity and compassion have not gone unnoticed by her critics, who have attempted to undermine her leadership style. Ardern says, 'One of the criticisms I've faced over the years is that I'm not aggressive enough or assertive enough, or maybe somehow because I'm empathetic, it means I'm weak. I totally rebel against that. I refuse to believe that you cannot be both compassionate and strong'.

Christina Boedker, a lecturer at the Australian School of Business, completed research on the correlation between leadership and organisational performance. Of the 5,600 people interviewed across 77 organisations, it was found that the combination of being an empathetic and compassionate leader had the biggest impact on profitability and productivity (Schneider, 2021). The understanding gained by being empathetic, when acted on, results in compassion, so they are intrinsically linked.

Tony demonstrated compassion.

We were really concerned for our colleagues and community. The floods had an emotional impact—not just for staff but for the whole community. It was fundamental to stay calm and centred, to have a clear vision, to show that we cared and to let people know there is hope and a way forward. We needed to be in tune with how people were feeling emotionally.

The impact of throwing everything out of someone's home before it turns into a mouldy toxic mess is just terrible. It's really difficult. You need to stay focused and be positive and remind people of the longer-term outcomes. We are going to be there for the community.

Acknowledging what a time it has been for people and communicating internally gives the greatest sense of security. As an organisation, how we drive culture and build connections is critical. We have a greater sense of safety and stability in a very changeable and unpredictable world.

I practise empathetic and secure-based leadership. Sometimes I'm successful and other times I haven't achieved what I intended. I need to constantly reflect on that. I think it's how people experience it that really counts.

Tony had to lead through a very challenging time. He needed to demonstrate empathy for the community and his team members who were directly and indirectly impacted. This is an extreme example, but every day we need to put ourselves in our team members' shoes and show compassion and empathy.

Adaptive leadership

According to Harvard professors Marty Linsky and Ronald Heifetz, adaptive leadership is anticipating challenges and root causes, and recognising risks and where an organisation should place its time (2010). Adaptive leadership means mobilising people to overcome challenges.

Leaders face technical challenges that can be addressed with a one-off solution that has generally been seen before. But leaders also face adaptive challenges that require systemic cultural shifts. Adaptive challenges are complex; they require listening and feedback loops, and observing and interpreting the situation. We must learn the way forward and make decisions based on our interpretations. This requires readiness and nimbleness to pivot and change direction. It also requires a level of comfort in ambiguity. The volatile and uncertain world we live in has required adaptive leadership more and more.

Tony had to demonstrate adaptive leadership.

When the floods hit, we were able to work remotely. During the COVID-19 pandemic, we underwent a rapid and urgent process to change our ways of working. We set ourselves up to be more disaster resilient.

It has been hard to have a clear plan and stick to that. Only a week or two before the floods, we said, 'We've made it through the pandemic'. Then it started raining.

Human services need a physical space. After the floods, we decided to not rebuild four sites but to look to have one location to build cohesion within the team. I had to get the message out nationally (about what was needed) to build awareness of the social and emotional consequences and the type of support Lismore required. I ensured that stakeholders and governments were aware of the situation. I connected decision-makers to the research on the impacts from the 2017 floods. And I got in touch with politicians and funders to support the rebuild so we could be responsive to the community.

Communication was critical to maintaining a strong sense of optimism that Lismore can come back from this. We experienced a higher level of chaos and volatility than expected. The fire season in 2019, the pandemic and now the floods. We have had to be very adaptable.

Tony was presented with several challenges—some never experienced before. It required him to interpret the situation, listen to others around him and pivot directions to adapt to the circumstances.

Adaptive leadership requires resilience. Resilience is our ability to bounce back from adversity, cope under pressure, adapt and grow. We have all had to be incredibly resilient and adaptable living through a global pandemic. This was demonstrated by Tony and the community during the floods. Resilient leadership helps others manage through disruptive challenges. Adaptive leadership also requires an empathetic lens to see things from other perspectives.

As an Executive Coach, leaders consistently come to me for help in managing their time more effectively, weighing up the demands put on them and having some form of work-life balance. It's a story that most organisations are experiencing—do more with fewer resources. With organisations under pressure, employees are left stretched. It's hard to sustain that tension. Add to this the external factors of natural disasters such as fires, floods and a global pandemic and it is a recipe for burnout. We need to practise self-care and compassion.

Building your leadership style

Irrespective of your leadership style, you need to build awareness and create an intention for how you want to lead. You can do this by building self-awareness, completing personality assessments, understanding your strengths, creating a leadership intention and establishing mentor relationships.

Self-awareness

Emotional intelligence is the ability to manage your own feelings and emotions and appropriately express them. It is also about understanding, interpreting and responding to the emotions of others. According to Daniel Goleman, who wrote the book *Emotional Intelligence,* the components that make up emotional intelligence are self-awareness, self-regulation, motivation, empathy and social skill. Goleman also cites Harvard Business School research, which states that emotional intelligence counts twice as much as IQ and technical skill (*Working with Emotional Intelligence*, 2009).

Self-awareness objectively interprets your emotions and feelings, which impacts your behaviours and actions. It also allows you to interpret how you are perceived by others, as often our intentions are different to how people experience us. The aim is to see yourself as others see you.

As leaders, we need to understand how our behaviours impact others. A leader's reactions are noticed. Self-aware people also have a deep understanding of their strengths and areas for development. We all have blind spots, and the more we can build awareness around these— through feedback and disclosing areas we are working on—the more we can bring them into our awareness.

Emotional intelligence and self-awareness can be developed and practised. The more you understand yourself, the better you can understand others.

Early in my career, I was part of a small People & Culture team at a large financial institution. I was the youngest and most inexperienced person in the team. The team leader, Liz Compton, was an impactful, authentic and introverted leader.

During each team meeting, I'd launch into a list of priorities I wanted to discuss with the team. In one meeting, in her very polite style, Liz said, 'If it's okay with you, Claire, I wanted to cover a few priorities first. Is that okay?' Immediately I realised how unperceptive I'd been in the meetings and that I needed to read the room and the situation. Looking back, I laugh at how little self-awareness I had about my role and the context of those meetings.

When I contacted Liz to ask if I could share this story, her response was, 'I think you are being a bit hard on yourself. Your energy and input was always well considered and added value'. This is proof that two people can have different interpretations of the same situation.

Personality

Personality plays a key role in how people think and feel. It affects many aspects of work. People's personalities influence their behaviours, attitudes, motivation and decision-making. The more you understand how personality impacts behaviour in the workplace, the better equipped you'll be to effectively achieve organisational goals.

However, before you can understand the personality styles of your team, you must understand your own personality style. It's vital you can confidently identify your personality style, your natural work preferences, your strengths, your areas for development, and what motivates and demotivates you. By understanding your own values and what truly drives you, you can seek to understand what drives those around you.

There are five fundamental building blocks of our personalities. They are extroversion, emotional stability, agreeableness, conscientiousness and openness to experience. We all possess these personality traits to different degrees. The differences create unique personalities.

Personalities stabilise when we reach our mid-20s; however, that doesn't mean traits can't continue to evolve. We have learnt behaviours that we put in place to be effective. In times of stress and change, these learnt behaviours go out the window and we default to our natural personality preferences.

Leaders need to manage different personality styles. You often assume that people are like you, but as you start to work in management, you soon realise different personality styles impact a team's dynamics and can make or break a team.

Differences in personalities can cause workplace conflict. Diverse backgrounds and experiences play a role in a team's dynamics. When employees fail to understand or accept our differences, problems arise. However, team diversity can be leveraged to create a cohesive high-performing team. Understanding your personality and adapting your leadership style to different behavioural styles takes practice and discipline. It means you must adapt how you communicate, delegate work, give feedback and coach. When leading, there is no one-size-fits-all formula. Adapting your style to match that of your team or team member is key.

I'm often asked if there is an ideal personality style for a strong leader. My answer is that great leaders come with different strengths and personality types. This is why understanding your authentic leadership style and what you bring to leadership is so important.

A great way to understand yourself is to take a personality assessment that offers you meaningful information with which you can work. This builds self-awareness.

Strengths

Historically, psychology was deficit-based and focused on surviving, weaknesses or problems. The positive psychology movement led by psychologists Martin Seligman and Mihaly Csikszentmihalyi focuses on strengths, happiness and flourishing. It helps build meaning and purpose in our lives and promotes wellbeing and improved quality of life (Ackerman, 2022).

Gallup (2021) analysis reveals that people who use their strengths every day are three times more likely to report having an excellent quality of life, six times more engaged at work, 8% more productive and 15% less likely to quit their jobs.

A strength is something that energises us. It is something we are good at. When we are feeling at our best, or in a state of 'flow', we are likely using our strengths. A flow state, as defined by Csikszentmihalyi, is when we are so immersed in an activity that we are completely absorbed by what we are doing and time flies by without us knowing.

Clifton and Harter (Gallup, n.d.) conducted a study in the 1950s with 6,000 Year 10 students to identify the value of speed reading. There were two groups: a norm group that could speed read at 90 words per minute and a gifted group that could speed read at

300 words per minute. They both completed the same training over three months and were tested again. What do you think happened? Drum roll please ... They both improved. The norm group improved by 67% speed reading at 150 words per minute. The gifted group improved by 867% speed reading at 2,900 words per minute. That's a pretty good business case to focus on the natural talents and strengths within your team.

The purpose of this study wasn't to explore strengths, it was the catalyst for Clifton to spend the rest of his life exploring and researching the power of strengths. The study demonstrated that focusing on natural talent means you can go from being good at something to being great—it becomes a strength.

As humans, our natural tendency is to focus on our weaknesses: going from not so great to mediocre. I'm not saying you shouldn't focus on *any* weaknesses but don't make this your sole focus. We often don't take the time to consider our natural talents and strengths. By leveraging the strengths of each team member and playing to everyone's strengths, the whole team will feel energised and in flow. Building a team with a complementary skill set is important. For example, a team with a visionary leader will often need operational implementors to execute their ideas. Understanding your strengths and the strengths of your team is important so everyone is operating at their best.

'Great leaders are not defined by the absence of weakness, but rather by the presence of clear strengths.'
—John Peter Zenger

What are your strengths?

Take some time to reflect on your strengths. You may want to create a list. If you want to understand your strengths, you can complete a survey that captures your strengths. The VIA Survey of Character Strengths (VIA Institute on Character) is based on the work of Christian Peterson and Martin Seligman. You can do a free survey that takes about ten minutes or a paid version with more insights. Gallup's Cliftons Strength Finder has a strengths diagnostic based on the work of Don Clifton. Both are great tools to understand your values and strengths because they look at your top signature strengths and your lesser strengths.

Knowing your strengths and how you can leverage them doesn't mean you need to use them all the time. Dr Alex Linley talks about a shadow side of strengths. This is when a strength is overused and becomes a weakness. We also underutilise strengths; perhaps we don't have the opportunity to use them at work. We need to understand how to use these strengths more or find outlets outside of work to make use of them. What doesn't come naturally to you? These may be actions that feel forced or make you feel de-energised. If it is something you don't perform well and it drains you, then it may be a weakness. If it is something you can perform well but makes you feel de-energised, it is likely a learned behaviour (Glabb, 2002).

We all have things we are not good at. Identify the things that de-energise you in your day. Work out what can be delegated to others. For things that are requirements in your role, determine who you could partner with to bolster up your lesser strength. The more energised we are in what we are doing, the more fulfilled we will feel.

Strengths are contextual and although you may have enduring signature strengths, they do change over time due to context.

Leadership intention

A leadership intention is your personal value proposition or elevator pitch. It describes your own journey, values, goals and expectations. By articulating your leadership intention, you can be a more authentic and intentional leader who inspires others.

Defining your intention as a leader is a powerful exercise. Here are some questions to reflect on before creating your leadership intention:

- What do you believe to be true about thriving leaders?
- What are your top three to five values when leading others?
- What gets in the way of you leading from your values every day?
- What are you most passionate about?
- What makes you a great leader?
- What type of leader do you aspire to be?

Once you have answered these questions, create a short paragraph (four to eight sentences) that describes who you are when you lead, your values and principles, your intentions as a leader and what your followers can expect of you.

Here are some sentence starters to help:

- My purpose is to …
- I have a vision to …
- By drawing on my strengths I …
- My values are …
- I have a passion for …
- I thrive when I …
- I am motivated by …
- I am known for …

Once you have documented your leadership intention, share it verbally with your team. This is a great way for your team to hold you accountable. It also models vulnerability.

Mentors

Having a support network is critical and having a mentor—or a few—can be beneficial. You can learn from their stories and experience and bounce your own ideas off them.

It is often helpful to have different mentors for different things. If you want to build your muscle in strategic thinking, consider who in your network does this well. If you need mentoring on leadership in general, reach out to someone with a different style to your own.

Jon Eddy has been my mentor for many years. My first interaction with Jon was when I was a participant on a talent program he facilitated. After that, he became my boss, then he was a mentor and now he is a friend. I call Jon 'the corporate Buddha'. He spent half his career as a sales leader in a financial institution and the second half of his career in leadership and team development. It's worth noting that I never asked Jon to be my mentor; it just happened naturally, and that is often the case. Jon and I have quite different personality styles, which is why I love his insight and wisdom—he brings a diverse perspective.

Having a strong mentor who can give you direct feedback, challenge you to think differently and help support your career development is important. It should be someone beyond your direct manager so there is some distance from the content you discuss.

The mentor-mentee relationship is reciprocal. You also add value to them, so make time to share your experiences. I've come across people who, for their own reasons, feel purposeful when they are supporting the development of others. Therefore, as the mentee, you are offering the mentor an opportunity to fulfil their purpose. It is also possible to have a reciprocal-mentor relationship where you are at a similar level with varied expertise. Sharing your experiences and diversity of thought can be really helpful.

When considering engaging a mentor, first ask yourself these questions:

- Do we share similar values?
- Would a mentor with different values and priorities to mine offer beneficial insights?
- Do I look up to them?
- Will they be able to provide me with insight, guidance and learnings?
- Will they challenge my thinking and ask tough questions?

Use your network to share the type of skill set or experience you are looking for in a mentor. Have a first meeting, coffee or virtual catch-up to see if there is a good connection and fit. At the end of the meeting, agree how you will catch up in the future. It may be monthly, bi-monthly or quarterly, or it may be on an ad-hoc basis. Keep up the momentum but understand that some mentor relationships come to a natural end. This is okay; it simply means they served their purpose well.

Who are your mentors? What value do they bring to you?

Confidence

If you want to feel more confident as a leader, you'll need to understand the expectations of you as a leader and define and adapt your leadership style to meet these expectations.

Confidence is the belief in yourself. We all experience self-doubt. According to a study from Queens University in Canada (2022), the average person has approximately 6,200 thoughts per day. Of these thoughts, 80% are negative and 95% are repeated. So, it is no wonder we feel levels of self-doubt, which can become our narrative and self-talk. Luckily, the brain is neuroplastic, meaning we can reprogram our brains to create more positive neural pathways through learning, experience and memory formation.

> *'The actions of confidence come first; the feelings of confidence come later.'*
> —Russ Harris

I love this quote by Russ Harris. Often, we wait to feel confident, but we might be waiting a long time. At times we need to act confident so that we can be confident. Building our skills and knowledge assists us to feel more confident. My hope is that *you* feel more confident as a leader by applying the techniques you learn in this book.

Imposter syndrome

Imposter syndrome, as the name suggests, is the feeling of self-doubt. You feel like a fraud or a phony. Your assumption may be that you landed your role through sheer luck.

We are often kinder to others than we are to ourselves. We can be our worst inner critics. When we listen to our inner critic, we feel like we are not good enough or we question whether we deserve our achievements. Some of the most confident leaders have experienced imposter syndrome—feeling at any moment, others will discover who they really are. For others, it can show up as a reluctance to accept positive feedback and praise from others.

It is reported that up to 82% of people experience imposter syndrome at some point in their lives (Leonard, 2020). If all your focus is on not being good enough, this could impact your performance. It will become a self-fulfilling prophecy. At its worst, it can impact your mental wellbeing and present with heightened levels of anxiety and depression. Conversely, in his book, *Think Again*, Adam Grant discusses three benefits of imposter syndrome:

- Motivation to work harder than everyone (giving it 110%).
- Being open to new ways of doing things.

- Becoming a better learner and seeking input and advice from others.

Ironically, while writing this book, I felt a sense of imposter syndrome. Seeds of doubt came into my head: *Who am I to write a book? I'm not an author. What if no one reads it? What if everyone reads it and it's no good?* I got over this by leaning on my support network. I reached out to my mentor to read a few chapters and instantly felt self-assured. Thanks, Jon! Dealing with imposter syndrome is partly about putting yourself out there knowing that you may fall rather than forever wondering *what if?* Lean on your support network when you are unsure.

Here is Tony's recollection of imposter syndrome.

When I first moved into leadership, I had far more of a sense of imposter syndrome. I felt I didn't know what I was doing and I was reluctant to take my own approach. I didn't want to rock the boat. And I was unwilling to hold people accountable.

Over time, I've become more confident in my approach and more willing to jump in and make a decision when one had to be made. I like to be consultative and that drives people mad at times. If I need to make a decision, I want to make the best possible decision and part of doing that is letting people have their say, even in the knowledge that ultimately, I'll make the decision.

My confidence has grown, as has my awareness that the important thing is to step in and act, make decisions and move forward. I must have a clear vision around what I'm trying to achieve and articulate it. I've also come to understand the value of culture as the prime enabler of delivering. I'm in the 'culture eats strategy for breakfast' camp. You need to have a strategy, but you know that culture is how you actually achieve a major change.

To overcome imposter syndrome, I think you just get in and do the work. Be open to asking questions. Get independent advice and have a sounding board.

Challenging limiting beliefs

Our beliefs are ideas we hold to be true. This may be based on a fact, opinion or assumption. Our beliefs are influenced by our perceptions, which become our reality.

Our thoughts are powerful because they control our emotions, and our emotions lead to our behaviours, what we act upon and how we react. Limiting beliefs are thoughts or opinions we believe to be the absolute truth. This has a negative impact and often restricts professional and personal growth. These boundaries and limitations hold us back. A common limiting belief is fear of failure—we're not good enough, we're not worthy of success.

Initially, you need to identify and question limiting beliefs. These may be obvious to you, but if you are unsure, ask a close friend, family member or colleague who knows you well. It is often easier to spot limiting beliefs in someone else than ourselves. Once your limiting beliefs have been identified, choose a new empowering belief, practise it in different situations and embed it through new ways of thinking and responding. Making a firm decision about changing limiting beliefs radically transforms you and builds confidence.

Reframing

If you are questioning your limiting beliefs, it's time to reframe your thoughts and change your mindset. If we visualise positive beliefs—like achievement and success—we can reframe and reprogram our neural pathways to automate and filter out information that contradicts the negativity.

A way to reframe unhelpful beliefs is to use the belief cycle. Our beliefs shape our mindset and our thought patterns. This impacts our emotions. Our feelings impact our behaviours, which when negative, result in an outcome we likely do not want. The outcome can then impact our beliefs and the cycle continues. If we can reframe our beliefs into something more positive, we will feel and behave differently, and we will likely see an optimistic outcome.

Unhelpful belief

Mindset: I'm not a good leader.

Feeling: I'm nervous and insecure.

Behaviour: I'm lacking in confidence and avoid difficult discussions.

Outcome: I don't perform well as a leader.

Reframe

Mindset: I'm becoming the leader I want to be.

Feeling: I feel authentic and genuine.

Behaviour: I'm calm, prepared and give things a go.

Outcome: I lead the team effectively.

Remember, you are not your thoughts. Believe in yourself. The belief cycle can also apply to our beliefs about people, which are not helpful. You may need to reframe an unhelpful belief you have about someone with whom you work.

Get comfortable with not being the smartest person in the room. Having the confidence to ask questions demonstrates humility. Draw on the strengths, wisdom and experience of the people around you.

Summary

There are opportunities to demonstrate leadership everywhere. Everyone can be a leader.

Thriving leaders are authentic. Authentic leadership is about becoming the leader you want to be. It's about finding the balance between the assertive, empathetic and adaptive parts of who you are. This requires you to read the situation and deploy the style that suits the context.

Reframe your self-doubt and turn it into opportunities. This is easier said than done; however, if you can embrace challenging experiences as learning opportunities, you will soon embrace this as a way to grow.

🗒️ Actions

- Complete a Personality Assessment to build self-awareness. Use the QR code below if you'd like to complete a Facet5 Personality Profile and debrief.
- Complete a VIA Character Strengths Survey or Gallup's Cliftons Strength Finder to understand your strengths and values in more detail. How can you use your strengths more each day?
- Keep a strengths journal. Track how you use your strengths. This can include overuse, underuse, different ways in which you have used your strengths, the context in which you use your strengths and how you felt when you were in flow.
- Find a mentor and catch up regularly.
- Create a leadership intention. Use the QR code below for a guided template.
- Reframe an unhelpful belief using the belief cycle.

https://www.thrivingculture.com.au/tlbook

CHAPTER 2

Thriving Teams

*'Connection is why we are here; it is what
gives purpose and meaning to our lives.'*
—Brené Brown

What is a high-performing team?

Before talking about high-performing teams, we need to be clear on what constitutes a team. A team is ' ... a small number of people with complementary skills, who are committed to a common purpose, performance goals and approach, for which they hold themselves mutually accountable' (*The Discipline of Teams*, 2015). Therefore, a high-performing team focuses on its common purpose and goals. Team members work together through strong relationships and shared accountability to deliver exceptional business results.

In his book, *The Five Dysfunctions of a Team*, Patrick Lencioni famously said, 'Not finance. Not strategy. Not technology. It is teamwork that remains the ultimate competitive advantage, both because it is so powerful and so rare'. Teamwork is real work. It is hard. It is messy. It requires tough conversations. It involves discomfort that drives us to be better for the greater good of the team. It is also fun, energising, empowering and inspiring to be part of a high-performing team.

Team dynamics

There will be a different dynamic in every team with which you work. Each team has its micro-culture based on the people in it, how they interact with each other and the outcomes they are trying to deliver. Each team member, including the leader, sets the tone for the team dynamic. Due to the power differential, the leader holds disproportionate weight in influencing that dynamic.

In most organisations, you are part of more than one team. Lencioni discusses the concept of your first or primary team. He suggests that your first team should be the team you are part of or the more senior team. If you assumed your first team is the team you lead—which most leaders do—your mindset could drive siloed behaviour. It is often the leaders in organisations who drive siloed behaviours where their focus is on looking after their patch rather than lifting their gaze and making decisions for the greater good of the organisation. Remember, 'first team mentality' is a concept: you still need to support and develop the team you lead. There is no room for 'us versus them'.

Politics in the workplace happens when employees have differences in opinions, power, personality styles and authority. Work politics influences social structures and individual behaviours. There is a risk of toxicity when people protect themselves to prove their relevance. Like when making an omelette and the last egg you crack into the bowl is bad—the whole mixture is spoiled. This is also true of your team's culture. This toxic environment causes stress and anxiety for everyone involved.

Many organisations have high-performing individuals. But until everyone is rowing in the same direction, there can be conflicting agendas. Egos, unhealthy competition and behaviours impact the team's performance. The team may be delivering results, but at what cost? A toxic team environment is not sustainable.

Diversity within a team drives innovation and new thinking. It reduces the likelihood of groupthink driven by a team's need for consensus and conformity, which detracts decision-making. Problems arise when employees fail to understand or accept the differences in each other's personalities. Diverse teams are often high-performing, but they also encounter barriers like differences in personalities, views and opinions—all of which can cause task conflict.

An example of task conflict would be one team member having an objective to reduce cost within the business and another team member having a growth and expansion objective. This task conflict causes tension as there are different opinions about goals. To overcome this, find shared values and a common purpose. Relationship conflict is a perceived interpersonal difference. Task conflict can lead to relationship conflict.

Being promoted into a leadership position can change the team's dynamic. You had established relationships with the team but now the power dynamic has shifted and the relationship from mate to manager followed. This can feel uncomfortable. You still want to be friends, you feel like you are pretending to be the leader, you feel exposed or uncomfortable as you need to be serious about things that weren't your responsibility until now. When I was promoted to lead the team, I was told, 'Sorry, we can't share this with you now as you're the boss'. I understood, but as a person who suffers from FOMO (fear of missing out), it felt lonely to be on the outside.

When you shift to leading your previous peers, you must establish new professional boundaries and re-establish working relationships. Having a conversation with each team member about your expectations and asking them to share their expectations of you can help redefine the working relationship.

What is your current team dynamic or culture? Is it supportive or competitive? Are there subcultures? It is helpful to discuss this openly with your team. Ask what they consider the culture to be and what they would like it to be. Then work on bridging the gap together.

Thriving Teams Model

The Thriving Teams Model is based on extensive experience creating effective teams, empirical research, evolving *good* practice (to quote David Clutterbuck—as there is no such thing as *best* practice) and thought leadership on high-performing teams.

There are three fundamental components of a thriving team:

- Purpose: why the team exists.
- Relationships: how the team works together.
- Accountability: what the team will achieve and by when.

The intersection between these components is equally as important. They are:

- Connection.
- Challenge and Support.
- Alignment.

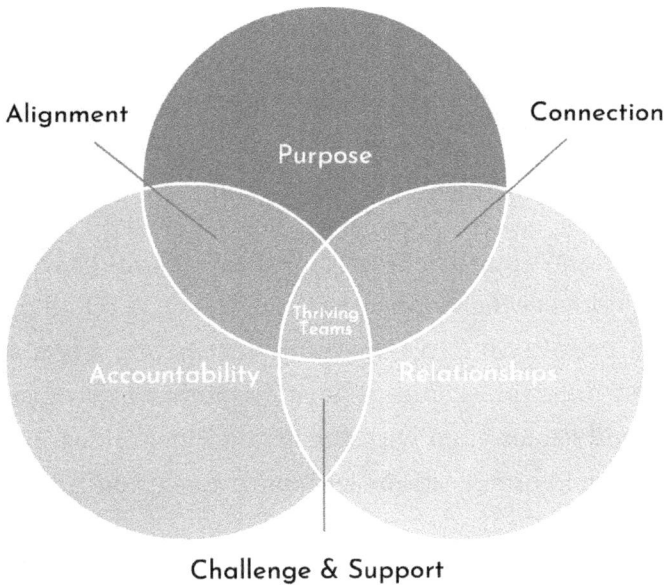

Purpose

Purpose relates to an intention, a long-term goal and a reason for being. The purpose is why you exist. It should be meaningful, aspirational and motivating. In the Thriving Teams Model, Purpose intersects with Alignment and Connection. This ensures the team has clarity and is aligned on its purpose. When the team connects, it is meaningful and purposeful.

There are four levels of purpose to which individuals can connect:

- The organisation's purpose.
- The team's purpose.
- Meaningful work.
- Personal values.

As leaders, we can influence the first three levels of purpose.

Organisational purpose

An organisation's purpose is why it exists. It should have meaning so that employees feel connected to it. The COVID-19 pandemic has given people time to reflect on what is important to them, to reassess their values and to decide whether the organisation's purpose and values align with their individual values. People are seeking work in organisations with purpose-led cultures.

What is your organisation's purpose? How are you connecting your team members to it?

Team purpose

A clear team purpose binds the team to a common 'why'. Almost all literature on high-performing teams describes the need for a collective purpose. The purpose defines team culture and describes why it exists. It links personal values, meaningful work and collective purpose.

Work with your team to articulate a team purpose statement. It should be one sentence that describes why your team exists. It should be inspiring. It should connect the team. A clear team purpose is key to a thriving team. Questions to help you develop a team purpose include:

- Why does our team exist?
- What legacy will our team leave?
- What differentiates our team from others?

Meaningful work

There aren't many people who come to work to do a bad job. Most people take pride in what they do. The more an individual can connect to the work and the value that their work provides, the more rewarding their work will be. As leaders, we need to make the connection to the impact of their work. This can be easier for people who work in areas where their impact is obvious, for example, health and environment. For less obvious fields, think about what motivates an individual. What drives them? What are their values? This will make it easier to make the connection.

It's important to note here that what drives *you* may not drive your team members. For example, you may be driven by learning and growth, whereas another team member may be driven by status and autonomy. Or a sales leader may be driven by lifestyle and reward, whereas a team member may be driven by family and learning. These may drive different behaviours.

Personal values

We each have core values that are important to us. These could be family, social, relational or environmental. Our values shape our decisions and influence our beliefs and assumptions. If you want to explore your values in more detail, complete the VIA Survey of Character Strengths as discussed in Chapter 1. Open the door to genuine dialogue, deliver more opportunities for people to find purpose in their work and make sure you're doing it authentically.

High-performing Koala

Koala.com is a successful direct-to-consumer furniture company, with operations in Australia, Japan and South Korea. The company has experienced rapid growth since its launch. It went from zero to $13 million in its first year in 2015, and by 2022 it is reported to be worth over $500 million. As innovators in their market, Koala disrupted an overpriced industry and introduced high-quality, affordable and sustainable online furniture. They offer a 120-night free trial to ensure customers are satisfied and they run a world-leading four-hour delivery service. You know when you are onto a good thing when so many other companies copy your innovation.

I'm keen to get under the sheets to understand what made this team so high-performing and learn the secret to their success. I spoke with Sandy Morrow, who felt privileged to be on the ride from the start as the former Head of Operations at Koala.com.

> *Koala is well known as a major disrupter in the Australian furniture industry, but what you might not realise is that we disrupted every element of business and threw out the traditional ways of working to allow us to scale without the limitations that corporates are faced with. If we truly wanted to*

change an industry, we needed to think, behave and lead our teams differently.

Koala was born as a profit-for-purpose start-up and supported Koala wildlife sanctuaries with significant donations from day one. Now, Koala partners with WWF and supports a number of wildlife initiatives across Australia. Social good was in our DNA from the beginning, it influenced how we treated the environment, our customers, our suppliers and of course our people.

High performance is easy with small, motivated start-up teams, and at Koala, it was the reason for our early success. Everyone knew what initiatives were priority and why, and they understood what part they played in the company's success. A small team meant we didn't have to consider how projects were communicated, nor did we need to map detailed timelines and task plans. It happened organically. As we scaled, maintaining high performance was challenging. We threw a lot of different strategies at our teams to maintain pace, of which accountability had a huge impact.

At Koala, we focused on communicating the why more so than the what. You can tell someone step by step what they need to do, and they will do it your way. When they understand why they need to do it, they will do it using their own initiative, often driving a better business outcome while empowering them.

Relationships

Relationships are critical to thriving teams. Relationships are how we interact and behave with each other. Nearly every study on team effectiveness highlights the importance of the quality of relationships. This doesn't mean you need to be mates or even like each other but there does need to be psychological safety, trust and a sense of belonging and inclusion for a team to thrive.

Thriving teams demonstrate care and compassion for one another as individuals and as a team. This is why Relationships intersects with Connection and Challenge and Support in the Thriving Teams Model.

I work with diverse teams to help them work most effectively together. When things aren't working as effectively as they could be, it signals that a team is either dysfunctional or wants to fast-track becoming an exceptionally high-performing team.

Psychological safety

Amy Edmondson describes psychological safety as, '...individuals' perceptions about the consequences of interpersonal risks in their work environment. It consists of taken-for-granted beliefs about how others will respond when one puts oneself on the line such as by asking a question, seeking feedback, reporting a mistake or proposing a new idea' (Conley, 2018). Team members won't be punished or humiliated when speaking up with ideas, questions, concerns or mistakes. In several of Edmondson's studies, she found that teams with high levels of psychological safety could speak openly, address difficult issues and manage conflict effectively. Psychologically safe teams learn from mistakes. Fear is not a barrier, so they take more risks, appreciate the diversity of thought and are more innovative.

In 2012, Google commenced Project Aristotle. The aim of the

research into 180 of Google's teams was to uncover the secret to a highly effective team. Why do some teams achieve so much while others coast along? The result was that psychological safety— feeling safe to take interpersonal risks and show vulnerability in front of your teammates—was the most important factor.

A dysfunctional team

A team within a large telecommunication provider had formed through a restructure. Team members were resisting the change and working in the old structure, engaging with their previous stakeholders and resisting the leadership of their new leader.

The team didn't identify as a team. There was no team purpose. Team members felt there was little alignment, and they didn't understand why they needed to work together. Their primary focus was the team they led and not the collective value of the broader team.

There was a lack of trust and psychological safety. The team didn't feel safe raising issues for fear of being shut down by their leader. Conversely, the leader's expectations were higher than what was previously expected of them. Everyone on the team was feeling a level of frustration and helplessness. There was a sense of 'us and them' between the leader and the rest of the team. This story is a common one.

According to Maslow's hierarchy of needs, belonging is a fundamental need. As humans, our brains are hardwired to belong (*A Theory of Human Motivation*, 2013). In 2019, BetterUp researched the value of belonging in the workplace. Their research found that when employees felt they belonged, they not only performed better but there was less turnover and fewer sick days, which impacts the profitability of an organisation. When we feel included:

- We feel valued.
- We can be our authentic selves.
- We feel trusted.
- We feel psychologically safe.

I'm sure you can relate to experiences where you felt you truly belonged and were included. It's also likely that you have experienced instances at work where you have felt on the outer: left out, rejected and not included. When we feel excluded or that we don't belong, it causes us to question relationships and plant seeds of doubt; we worry, become anxious, fear being rejected and create competitive behaviours.

As leaders, we need to create space for building a sense of belonging. We must ensure that each team member feels included and that they are valued and respected.

How to build psychological safety with your team

When a team has psychological safety, it can lead to conversations that drive innovation, push boundaries and challenge habitual thinking. When people feel fearful or unsafe, they will not speak up.

The HBR article, *High-Performing Teams Need Psychological Safety*, suggests that to create psychological safety you need to create mutually desirable outcomes, personalise communication, anticipate reactions and plan responses, and trade blame with curiosity.

Ways to build a psychologically safe environment:

- Create opportunities for generative dialogue and reflection within the team about how things are going. What's working well? What can be improved? How vulnerable has the team been on a scale from 1–10?
- Ask team members how safe they feel on a scale from 1–10? What could the team do collectively to make the environment feel safer?
- Role model vulnerability. Share where you have made mistakes and what you have learnt in the process. Encourage others to share.
- If psychological safety is something you are concerned with, find a team coach to support you and the team to create a high-performing team environment.
- Reflect on whether there are behaviours you are demonstrating that are making team members feel excluded.

There is often confusion about the difference between psychological safety and trust. Psychological safety is based on what is happening right now for the team; it involves the whole team and is based on collective team norms. Trust occurs between two people; it is based on one-to-one, individual relationships.

Trust

Lencioni says the foundational pillar of any high-performing team is trust (2019). As leaders, we need to demonstrate vulnerability and build trust and genuine relationships with our team. This doesn't mean sharing your deepest, darkest secrets, it's about showing your human and empathetic side. If team members don't trust one another, fear becomes a driver of communication, and they become hesitant about being honest and open with each other and unwilling to take responsibility for fear of making mistakes.

When you are part of a great team, each member trusts everyone on an emotional level; they are comfortable showing vulnerability and sharing mistakes or weaknesses. Team members who trust each other are open with one another because they are confident that the individual has their best interests, and the team's, at heart.

> 'Vulnerability is not winning or losing;
> it's having the courage to show up and
> be seen when we have no control over the
> outcome. Vulnerability is not weakness;
> it's our greatest measure of courage.'
> —Brené Brown

This goes beyond trusting an individual's words spoken; it is the ability to form trust based on vulnerability. It means telling people when you don't have the answer or when you don't understand something—without fear of being judged. When employees trust you at work, they will go that extra mile, listen better and forgive more readily. When trust is low, there is fear, resistance and the potential for a breakdown in communication.

Elements of trust

The 4 Cs of Trust, which I have adapted from the work of

Trust and Betrayal in the Workplace (Reina & Reina, 2000) are communication, character, capability and consistency. When these four elements align, you are on the path to a high-trust environment.

Communication

Trust in communication means being able to share knowledge and information transparently, giving and taking constructive feedback, listening to learn, and speaking truthfully and with good intention. Communication creates clarity and certainty about where you stand with a team member regarding shared work and commitments.

Character

Trust of character is about integrity and common understanding between people. This is earnt over time and includes behaviours such as delegating appropriately, admitting mistakes, apologising, preserving confidentiality, maintaining boundaries and showing vulnerability. It means being honest about results and expectations and following through on commitments.

Capability

This is the trust others invest in you due to their confidence in your competence. Trust is demonstrated when you acknowledge skills and abilities and recognise these strengths. You need to be open, value others' input and help them learn new skills. It stretches beyond your current capabilities and presumes confidence that you will learn and develop new capabilities in the future.

Consistency

Reacting in a predictable way and committing to promises you make gives people reassurance. Be stable in your approach, follow through on promises and ensure your words match your actions.

Model consistent communication, character and capability.

How to build trust with your team

We are all human. We don't always take the time to connect with each other when we are at work. People want to feel seen and heard. Trust occurs after time spent together. There are several exercises you can perform to help build trust and fast-track that time.

Find opportunities for team members to share more about who they are. Set aside the first five minutes of team meetings for a non-work-related check-in. Change up the topics to include best holiday ever, worst holiday ever, favourite foods, movie recommendations, what happened on the weekend, what everyone's binging on Netflix or favourite books.

When you have more time—and at least on a quarterly basis— these simple group activities help the team to get to know each other on a personal level.

- Share a personal story and how it has shaped you as a leader. Then get others to share.
- Share career-defining moments.
- Create a life-on-a-page where people stick photos on a page and share what the pictures mean to them.

- Get everyone to bring in an object that is meaningful to them. Let them share why.
- Get everyone in your team to complete the free VIA survey and share their top five strengths. Discuss synergies and differences within the team.
- For more rigour using a personality or behavioural diagnostic, use a team report to help create a platform for a discussion about how effectively the team is working together and how natural behavioural styles help or hinder the team's effectiveness.
- Eat together; enjoy a team breakfast, lunch or dinner.
- Have a fun team gathering: yoga, meditation, a puzzle panic room, painting class, team volunteering, a beach clean, an amazing race scavenger hunt through the city. Just think of something that will include everyone.

It can be more challenging to build trust with a team that has been newly formed or is working apart from one another. Be more conscious to create these opportunities to build trust.

Teams are always evolving; people come and go, work changes and priorities shift. Ensure that when you bring new team members into the team, share the journey that you have been on— challenges and successes. Buddy them up and ensure a robust onboarding process. If there is a strong team culture, they may feel on the outer. Be conscious to bring them into the fold; be open to their ideas and suggestions rather than closing them down with 'we tried that before and it didn't work'.

Trust within hybrid teams requires a level of autonomy. When employees have autonomy to decide how the work should be done, it creates engagement and retention. This means leaders need to manage for outcomes and not hours.

> To be a disruptor and innovate a market sector as Koala did, there needs to be strong relationships, psychological safety and trust.
>
> Start-ups are not for the faint-hearted as they scale the demands on people and leadership continuously changes. At Koala, we prepared our teams for this by communicating that change is good and inevitable, and we should expect the business to feel completely different every six months. If the business was to grow +100% year on year, then as humans and leaders, we needed to follow that same growth trajectory. For some, this was a hard concept, and many great people would flounder when faced with start-up ambiguity and fast pace.
>
> Internally we'd say, 'We fail with enthusiasm today to achieve greatness tomorrow'.
>
> To drive growth in a start-up, you must be willing to take risks, to try different initiatives and be willing to fail. This is hard unless you can embody a growth mindset, where you understand that failure is learning, and learning is growth. We always focused on a fail fast approach. For this to work, we had to create a safe environment where team members were encouraged to step outside of their comfort zones, test and fail. We shared our stories, successes and failures at town hall meetings to celebrate those who won, and most importantly, those who tried.
>
> As a leadership team, we were sometimes faced with power struggles and misalignment. It wasn't always easy, but to thrive as a team, we used vulnerability to build trust. Through trust,

we were able to build a high-functioning team. And through leadership team coaching, we shared personal stories, ate together and broke down barriers by showing vulnerability.

Accountability

Accountability is delivering on commitment, using initiative to follow through and taking responsibility for an outcome. Accountability intersects with Alignment and Challenge and Support in the Thriving Teams Model. Accountability within a team is 'what' you will achieve and by 'when'.

In the context of a team, a lack of accountability can happen when there is no clear vision of where you are heading or committing to too much rather than defining what is most important. The team must have clear expectations of what is expected from a performance and a behaviour perspective. Clear expectations allow teams to hold one another accountable and ensure the team has a common goal.

(We will dive into your role as a leader, setting clear expectations and holding your team accountable in Chapter 5.)

Clear direction and expectations

A strategy is a big picture, it's a long-term view of what you want to achieve as a team. This clarity of direction alleviates ambiguity and confusion about where you are headed. Once you are clear on the strategy, you can determine how to operationalise the strategy by setting goals to get there. You will have long- and short-term goals. It is important to be clear about what success looks like if you achieve those goals. (I share models to help with this in Chapter 5.)

Be open and share your expectations with your team. Ambiguity can lead to underperformance and slow decision-making. When expectations aren't clear, it is more difficult to hold people accountable.

When your team has a clear direction and an understanding of how each person contributes towards it, they are aligned. The more involvement the team has in creating the strategy and setting the goals and plan, the more buy-in they will have to achieve the shared goals. Teams work most effectively when everyone understands, endorses and commits to the team's shared goals. Commitment enables teamwork with focused effort and attention, rather than individual interests. Just like a game of tug of war, if the team members aren't pulling in the same direction, the strength of the overall team is limited. Clarity ensures everyone understands the decisions, agreements and direction of the group.

Leaders can ensure the team is focusing on results by developing and implementing mechanisms that encourage them to do so: clear objectives, transparent results and linking recognition to achieving results. Provide meeting agendas with outcomes to be achieved to keep employees prepared and on track. Be clear on what you want regarding collaboration, how feedback is given and received, and overall performance.

Hold each other accountable

Thriving teams hold one another accountable without the need to be driven by the leader. Lencioni shares that, 'accountability can be achieved when the team members demonstrate a commitment to agreed standards of performance and decisions'. Teams will share accountability voluntarily and ensure other team members stick to those decisions and standards. This frees leaders from being the sole provider of accountability and team members can rely on each other to monitor each other's performance. It is difficult to hold individuals accountable for their part of a decision or agreement if they have not contributed to the decision-making process, do not have buy-in or lack clarity on the desired outcomes.

In Project Aristotle, the team discovered that 'dependability' was the second most important factor in determining team effectiveness. This is about completing work on time, taking responsibility and delivering high calibre results. To do this in a high-performing team, you must hold each other accountable.

This does not shirk the leader's responsibility or get them off the hook. In high-performing teams, it is the responsibility of every member to hold each other accountable.

Connection

Connection is about having meaningful and purposeful reasons to connect and having simple team processes and ways of working. It also creates opportunities for non-work-related conversations to build relationships and team cohesion.

Team processes

Thriving teams have meaningful and purposeful connections.

They create opportunities for the team to come together and discuss what is important. They collaborate with purpose. They have meaningful content to share, make decisions on, problem-solve and collaborate.

Developing ways of working lets people know what to expect. How do you ensure the team meets with purpose? What is the operating rhythm? What is the purpose for the meeting? Is it to make a decision, share information or solve a problem?

Teams can sometimes get tied down with prescriptive meeting agendas. Should meetings have agendas? Hell yes. However, if you are in a senior position, you need to ensure there is space to collaborate and problem solve—and this needs space on the agenda. The opposite normally happens, however, where meetings are filled with papers, approvals and signoffs. Be clear on whether the meeting is operational or strategic. Does the meeting require strategic problem-solving or creative brainstorming? If so, you need time.

This topic is even more interesting with the move to hybrid work. Navigating this transition has been challenging with the variance in people wanting to work from home, hybrid and/or in the office. It takes strong leadership, a team culture of purpose, and relationships with a strong focus on trust and accountability to manage hybrid work effectively.

When employees who work in a hybrid environment come into the office, they need it to be a valuable, exciting and meaningful experience. The Microsoft Annual Work Trend Index (2022) indicates that 38% of employees reported it is not clear when or why they should come into the office. We need to meet with purpose.

Have simple team processes, a strong operating rhythm and ways of working that are understood by all members of the team. These should be reviewed every three to six months to ensure they are effective. Leaders of thriving teams must prioritise connection and team empowerment over micromanagement and control. Create opportunities for collaboration and connection.

Togetherness

Togetherness is the quality time you spend together as a team. It is also how you spend time when you are not physically together, for example, virtual interactions and phone calls.

Peter Hawkins, in *Leadership Team Coaching*, talks about connection being beyond just the time you spend together as a team—it is also about what you do and how you behave when you are not together. Consider how one team member represents the whole team when they engage with a stakeholder. They are not just representing themselves. How do you talk about your team members when you engage with stakeholders? It is important that the team acts as a team, speaks with conviction about and supports their fellow team members when they are together and apart. You must be a team regardless of your physicality.

Relationships are built when we are together, but we don't always have the luxury of spending time face to face. High-performing teams communicate regularly even if they are not together. Appreciating different styles and understanding and valuing our differences creates an inclusive team. Inclusion develops the feeling of belonging. Team members feel valued, respected and heard. Be open to varying communication styles and set the tone for things that may not be appropriate culturally for the team, rather than just in your opinion.

Ways to create togetherness include:

- Be open to others' perspectives.
- Respect diversity of thought.
- Come from a place of curiosity.
- Ask questions and seek to understand rather than assume you have all the answers.
- Show respect and treat people as individuals.

We are all taught to 'be professional', but we don't need to be less human as a result.

Challenge and Support

Thriving teams have challenging debates. They can manage conflict healthily. They have hearty discussions where they get everything out on the table for the greater good of the team. They appreciate diversity of thought. They challenge with a supportive intention that drives robust ideas and team growth. Thriving teams also support each other. They ask for help when they are struggling and don't feel they will be reprimanded or judged for doing so. Thriving team members have each other's backs.

Healthy debate

Passionate discussions. Arguing or yelling. Not saying what's on your mind. These are some of the different dynamics that can happen within teams.

Psychological safety and trust need to be in place for teams to challenge each other constructively and have passionate debates around issues and decisions that are key to the team's success. Members of a high-performing team will challenge, question and disagree with the intent of finding the best decision for the team.

Lencioni says, 'all great relationships, the ones that last over time, require productive conflict in order to grow'. In 'nice' and 'harmonious' working cultures, leaders have simply created a layer of politeness over a layer of fear. They would rather be nice than offend or hurt others' feelings. Issues get stepped over as people avoid disagreeing. Conversely, teams who argue for the sake of having their opinions heard are driving their own agendas. Most people want to avoid conflict, but this may restrict your team from performing at their best and you are likely to miss out on honest communication, innovation and pushing boundaries.

Ways to encourage debates include:

- Create an environment where your teams feel safe to openly collaborate and embrace constructive debate.
- Model behaviours to challenge the status quo and generate new ideas. This will encourage others to face any fear of speaking up and being judged or ridiculed.
- Create a cultural expectation of healthy conflict by rewarding and protecting those who speak up, share their point of view and have bold ideas.

Healthy confrontations and conflicts are honest, open and goal directed. As such, they serve to improve the performance of the team or organisation. When teams are thriving, decisions are made in service of the team rather than your own agenda or ego.

Is what I'm asking the team in the best interest of the team or me?

Learning

Support can come in many shapes and sizes. Thriving teams need to know that their teammates will follow through on commitments. When there are trusting relationships, team members feel comfortable sharing if they are not meeting deadlines, if they do not have the capability and need the complementary skill set of the team. Being able to rely on one another for support brings strength to the team.

Teams learn just as individuals do. In his book, *Coaching the Team at Work,* David Clutterbuck shares several types of team learning: learning related to the tasks and processes, collective learning around the team's mindset, individual learning and unlearning. Learning as a team needs to be 'conscious, purposeful and directly related to the accomplishment of the team purpose'. It is important to create this reflective dialogue as a team, so you learn, grow, adapt and evolve. Individuals and the team develop in parallel. Team learning requires psychological safety as people need to be vulnerable and not fear taking risks.

Learning also happens between individuals of a thriving team. Team members need to build one-to-one relationships and trust with their colleagues.

How do your team members challenge and support each other?

Alignment

Alignment of goals enables strategy. Alignment is the commitment to the way forward for the organisation or team. It requires clarity on expectations and understanding the direction of the organisation for the team and with internal and external stakeholders.

Team

In thriving teams, team members can disagree and have diverse viewpoints—this promotes creativity and innovation. Alignment does not mean agreement. It means there is a commitment to the way forward where the team needs to be aligned and have a united front. There are no side conversations, meetings after meetings or comments against the direction.

Ensure you build in time for the team to have healthy debate in your operating rhythm and time to get clarity and commitment to the way forward, so the team is aligned and can speak with conviction about the direction more broadly. The team must be aligned to the purpose and direction through shared goals.

Stakeholders

Organisations are complex adaptive systems. Everything is interconnected. The team does not work in isolation. Some of the external pressures include parallel work, processes, matrix models, and relationships between teams and with internal and external stakeholders. Considering the impact of external factors, pressures and influences are important when understanding a high-performing team.

Peter Hawkins and David Clutterbuck discuss how teams don't work in isolation—they are part of complex adaptive systems. This means they must commission requirements from stakeholders and have relationships outside of the team. This applies if you are the most senior leadership team in an organisation with external stakeholders or if you are a team within the organisation with internal stakeholders. We must gain alignment and clarity in terms of expectations with stakeholders as this affects the team's ability to perform at its best.

The type of relationship, the way in which you engage and how you get aligned with stakeholders will be different depending on the stakeholder.

Sandy shared some secrets to their success.

At Koala, we created our company values by articulating the expectations we had on our team members and by embodying what we believed were the core traits of high performance.

- You are ambitious.
- You are curious.
- You are selfless.

We also encouraged independent decision-making. To enable this, we shared a list of belief statements that allowed team members to understand business decisions across a variety of areas. The more people could understand how we made decisions as an organisation, the more confidently they could make decisions and be empowered—that is high performance.

At Koala, we always got clear on our objectives with major stakeholders. The most important thing was to ensure each party understood what everyone is at the table for. It meant understanding everyone's objectives so there were no surprises.

Some teams are nervous about sharing bad news, but this is what allows you to work through it, understand objectives and find a solution that works for everyone.

We had open dialogue in our leadership meetings. We often used the group to problem solve, learn and bounce ideas. We didn't have a lot of heated arguments. Although those that we did have usually addressed the problem quickly and often resulted in a productive outcome. If we sit and dwell, the problem gets magnified.

Being able to communicate when you have been triggered by a peer and bring it to the surface is a challenging learning. At that moment, you are driven by emotion, ego and you are out of alignment. Take a breath, be aware of your impact and, once you have your emotions in check, address the issue. It's much easier to communicate with your leader than your peer. 'I may have reacted poorly, and I apologise' is a hard place to get to for most people.

Having 1:1s with your peers during challenging times can be super beneficial. It can be isolating being a leader: how do you navigate challenging people problems without undermining your team member? I learnt so much from my peers who had a completely different skill set and their view was often very helpful.

Thriving teams have a clear team purpose and strong relationships through psychological safety and trust. They are accountable to each other and aligned on the direction. They connect in a meaningful way, and challenge and support each other.

High-performance cultures

Culture is the vibe in an organisation. It is what it feels like to be part of a team. Culture is the collective beliefs, assumptions and values that drive how you do things. It is the cultivated behaviour patterns, interactions and social norms within the organisation or team.

Culture is intangible but can be observed in the way people communicate and make decisions, in how and when they send emails, where they sit in the office and how they act and behave when they are together. It is learned and shared with and through the people who are a part of it. Culture is also demonstrated through the behaviours that are tolerated or discouraged.

A high-performance culture is built on values, behaviours and norms within an organisation that makes it effective and productive and creates value that results in excellent business outcomes.

Values

Every organisation has values. They are demonstrated in the assumption and beliefs that lead to how people behave. Articulating the aspirational values of an organisation helps people understand what is valued and behaviours to be demonstrated. If your organisation hasn't developed values, then this is a good place to start. Ensure you engage employees in the process to develop meaningful values. I'd recommend trying to stick to three core values (no more than five), as you want them to be memorable. Next, define the behavioural descriptors that demonstrate these values. The values become the guiding principles for every employee within the organisation, so they know how to behave.

It is one thing to create values, but what matters is how you bring them to life in everything you do. Leaders need to rally their teams and role model the organisation's values and behavioural expectations, so they become more than words on a wall. Build this into your whole employee life cycle: from how you recruit employees who demonstrate your values to how you measure and reward performance and behaviours that align to your values in existing employees. Reward and recognition should be centred on the values.

Communicate your purpose and values regularly.

Employee experience

The 2022 study by Gallup found that only 17% of Australian employees are engaged compared to 21% globally. This means that globally, 79% of employees are either actively disengaged or not engaged. The study found a strong correlation between engagement and performance such as retention, productivity, safety and profitability (engaged teams are 23% more profitable). So how will you ensure that more of your workforce is engaged at work?

The employee experience describes every interaction an

employee has across the whole employee life cycle. From the recruitment experience to the day they start, how they are managed for performance, how they are developed, how they are communicated to, how they make decisions, how you react when they resign, through to the day they leave.

Employees have reported that what is most important to them is a positive work culture, health and wellbeing, a sense of meaning and purpose, and flexible hours (Work Trend Index, 2022).

> *'Those who build great organisations make sure they have the right people on the bus and the right people in the key seats.'*
> —Jim Collins

Invest the time in a solid recruitment process that selects people who align to the values of the organisation, have the right motivational and cultural fit, as well as the knowledge and experience.

Research shows 80% of a business's profits are generated by 20% of its workers—high-achieving A-players (Berglas, 2006). Take the time to further develop your talent and retain your high performers. Make it clear to these employees how they can progress within the organisation in terms of their career path and being future successors to key roles. Ensure you provide them with stretch opportunities, especially if you are in a smaller organisation where there may be a perceived ceiling. What can you delegate so they continue to feel motivated and challenged?

Measure how engaged your team is through employee engagement surveys. They give you insights into how the team feels so you can take meaningful action.

Listening and taking action

Kate Whitehill was newly appointed into her role within the healthcare industry in the UK. By listening to an internal employee engagement survey within the organisation, she immediately addressed negative feedback that was within her control. Within six months, she increased the engagement survey results by 35%.

Kate took on board the employee feedback, which was a staff shortage, no action being taken and a lack of career progression for employees.

What actions did Kate take?

- *She immediately commenced a recruitment drive with an approach that ensured the organisation selected the 'right' people for the roles based on cultural fit and capability.*

- *She increased support and structure around onboarding and checking in more frequently for feedback.*

- *She made herself more accessible as a listener.*

- *She empowered colleagues to make decisions.*

- *She implemented a meaningful training program for the team to support career progression.*

What were the results?

- *Her colleagues felt heard and more comfortable about approaching her with issues or feedback. They started working together to find the root cause of the problems.*

- *Her colleagues were happier and more engaged (35% which is a significant uplift).*

- *Team morale improved and the department is now 'one team' working with a more collaborative approach.*

Kate remained open-minded to new ideas and provided psychological safety for her colleagues to trust her and be confident to speak up.

Without change, things can't improve. You need to be open to it and use surveys and feedback as a tool to improve. It all starts from the top—if leaders can implement a feedback culture where people are seen, heard and valued, it results in higher performance.

A friend and client, Steve McEwin, says, 'When you are a leader of a high-performing team, you are like a gardener; your job is to create the environment for your team to excel—just like a gardener provides all the nutrients and water and removes the weeds so their plants can flourish'.

I encourage you to think about how you create the environment for your team to flourish.

Summary

A thriving team knows why they exist, how to work together, what to work on and when a task needs to be achieved.

A thriving team has a clear team purpose, strong relationships through psychological safety and trust, and members are accountable to each other. They are aligned and connected, and they will challenge and support each other to achieve their team and organisation's outcomes.

High-performance cultures anchor to their values and focus on their employee experience.

📝 Actions

- Discuss the Thriving Teams Model with your team. Use the QR code below to download questions to explore as a team. Have the team assess how efficient they are in the following areas. Then discuss which elements they would like to collectively focus on to improve.

  o Purpose – a clear team purpose and connecting to meaningful work.

  o Relationships – psychological safety and trust.

  o Accountability – clear direction and hold each other accountable.

  o Connection – team processes and togetherness.

  o Challenge and Support – healthy debate and learning.

  o Alignment – team and stakeholders.

- Create a team purpose with your team. Discuss how team members' values align to the team's purpose to build trust and alignment.

- Connect your team members to the work they do so it is meaningful and they understand the value they provide.

- Build trust by connecting and sharing personal stories. Get to know your team members on a personal level. What drives them? What are their strengths? What motivates them and what frustrates them? Role model vulnerability with your team.

- Define team shared goals. We will cover more on this in Chapter 5. Discuss alignment as a team to these goals and stakeholder expectations.
- Articulate simple team processes and ways of working so that the operating rhythm is clear. Meet with purpose and encourage healthy debate.

https://www.thrivingculture.com.au/tlbook

PART 2

Empower and develop your team

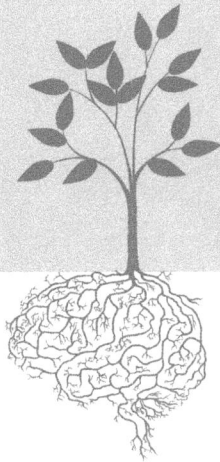

Think of a time when you were led by someone and felt completely empowered. How were you being led? Did you feel trusted?

Did you have autonomy to deliver an outcome? Did you receive helpful feedback that you could implement?

To empower your team members, create opportunities where they feel stretched, challenged and proud of what they can achieve. Let them shine.

Just as a sports coach provides feedback that motivates their players, a leader provides feedback and coaching that empowers and develops their team members. This is the winning formula in your leadership playbook.

It's time to get practical and dive into the art of feedback. We will explore how to deliver and receive feedback and what actions to take when faced with difficult conversations. We will build the skills to empower your team members by taking a coaching approach that asks powerful questions so they can solve their own problems.

CHAPTER 3

Feedback

*'The growth and development of people
is the highest calling of leadership.'*
—Harvey S. Firestone

What is feedback?

Feedback is the ability to let people know how they are doing. By providing information or data points, individuals can build self-awareness and make choices around behaviour change. Feedback can be positive to reinforce the behaviour you want to see more of or it can be constructive. Constructive feedback helps people learn and grow so they can understand where they made mistakes and where they could improve or try something in another way for a different result.

When some people hear the word feedback, the hairs on the back of their neck stand on end. You may have had a bad experience receiving feedback or perhaps you gave someone feedback and it didn't land as you intended. When feedback is delivered well, it leads to improved performance.

To nurture a feedback culture, leaders need to create a psychologically safe environment for their staff, where employees are willing to give honest feedback without ramifications. As a thriving leader, you will need to give and receive feedback.

Barriers to giving feedback

What gets in the way of giving feedback? There are several different reasons why people avoid having difficult conversations.

Some of these reasons include the following.

Affecting relationships

Leaders avoid feedback because they are concerned it will adversely affect their relationship with their team members—relationships that are critical for a thriving team. They don't want to come across as confrontational or unlikeable and difficult discussions often appear to be against that desire. As a team member, giving feedback to the leader could cause concerns due to their positional power.

Relationships can be strengthened and improved when feedback is delivered well. It is a sign that you care for the other person. When we stay silent and don't face feedback or hold others accountable, it can have a negative impact on our relationships as we start to feel resentment, frustration or lose respect for the other person. This will result in unintentionally destroying the relationship.

The quality of relationships and organisational performance improves when people learn the skills to have difficult conversations. By having feedback conversations, you will strengthen your relationships.

Reactions and feelings

Another reason for not facing difficult discussions is that you feel uncomfortable about how the other person might feel when you give the feedback. You may fear their reaction. Will it hurt their feelings? Will they be defensive? Will they be angry? Will they shut down?

However, if your intent is to help them learn and grow from the feedback, the way in which you provide it will be different than trying to highlight their shortcomings. Our natural personality style affects our ability to have difficult conversations. For example, people who are low on confrontation naturally find it more difficult to have challenging conversations. Luckily, this is a skill that can be learned.

Too busy and timing

Leaders are busy and time is always the most lacking resource. Some leaders get into a busy cycle. They wear the 'being busy' badge of honour and when it comes to feedback, they feel it is time-consuming. It requires preparation and practice. However, it creates more work in the long run if they don't address issues when they occur as they either happen again or are exacerbated.

Finding the right time can also be difficult, especially when we work in hybrid and remote environments. Too much time can pass before we are face to face with a person, and feedback via email or instant messaging doesn't land well because words get misinterpreted.

Timing is critical. Feedback should take place closely after the situation has occurred. Delaying this communication will dilute the effectiveness and relevance to the team member. So don't hold off.

Is it necessary?

Determining whether the feedback is warranted can be another reason for avoiding it. We can second-guess whether we really need to be delivering the feedback, especially when it is ambiguous or third hand.

In *Crucial Accountability*, Patterson discusses deciding whether the issue is worth bringing up and that the purpose of the discussion should be to maintain a positive and productive relationship with the other person. If you feel the conversation won't reach this goal, you need to work out how you will cope or get past the issue.

You need to reframe your belief and mindset about feedback from a negative inner dialogue to one where, as a leader, it is your role, obligation and privilege to hold the mirror up to your team, so they improve, learn and grow—personally and professionally.

If you have the right skills to formulate the discussion and you prepare carefully, you are more likely to have a successful conversation.

How do you feel about feedback?

A HBR study revealed that 44% of leaders believed that giving negative feedback was stressful and difficult. And 21% admitted they avoid giving negative feedback (Folkman & Zenger, 2017).

What might surprise some people is that they also discovered that 37% of leaders don't give positive reinforcement.

Sometimes, depending on how we feel about receiving positive feedback, we might be less likely to give positive feedback. This may be reflective of how we were raised. Did our parents or caregivers readily provide us with praise when we did things right? Or was the focus on when we did something wrong? I encourage you to reflect if this is a barrier for you.

In further research by HBR, they discovered that leaders are seen as more effective when giving praise. If you want to be a thriving leader, an immediate action is to try noticing when your team members are doing something right and provide positive feedback. You will be perceived as more effective.

Passive cultures are ineffective

As an all-male leadership team within the transport industry—an industry that is perceived to be quite macho—this group of men was spiritual and down to earth.

The founders had a strong friendship that was forged years before, but these relationships were starting to fracture based on their differing ideologies regarding how the business could be run.

There were frustrations with how others were working but no conversations were had—a 'nice' culture had developed and they all wanted to avoid confrontation. On face value, a nice culture sounds like something you would want. However, this led to conversations happening behind people's *backs, and the feedback and difficult conversations that needed to be faced for the greater good of the team were being avoided. This nice and passive culture was causing the team to be ineffective, and it impacted the overall performance of the business. Often, organisations spend a lot of time focusing on being productive and removing waste, when in fact, a lot of waste happens from conversations that haven't been had.*

How to give feedback

It is important to understand the fundamental principles of delivering feedback and the areas to watch out for.

Specific

The worst feedback you can give is, 'Good job'. Although it is positive, there isn't a lot someone can do with it in terms of replicating the positive behaviour. A better example might be, 'You did a great job today. You not only analysed the data, but you also provided your insights, which added value to the client'.

Feedback must be specific so it can be understood. The person receiving feedback must be able to learn from it and do something with it if they choose. This could be repeating the behaviour in a positive feedback scenario or adjusting or modifying their behaviour in a constructive conversation.

What is the critical message you need to get across? Vague conversations are confusing, so be specific. Come prepared with examples of where that behaviour or situation has been demonstrated.

Timely

Ensure you find the right place and time for difficult conversations. As the old saying goes, 'Praise publicly, criticise privately'. If you are providing constructive feedback, find a quiet, private place for the discussion. When criticism is delivered in a public forum, it belittles that person and will often reflect negatively on the leader. It can also cause other team members to withdraw out of fear of also being reprimanded in front of their peers.

An exception to this rule is if you are in a high-performing team with an extremely high level of psychological safety and trust and if the feedback is delivered in a way that doesn't make anyone feel singled out. The other exception is if there is team-wide feedback that needs to be given.

Praise, on the other hand, should be celebrated. As a thriving leader, reinforcing positive behaviours and deliverables to set a high-performance standard is important. Just be mindful of spreading the love, as only singing the praise of one consistent high performer may have a negative effect on the rest of the team.

Ideally, feedback should be face to face, but don't use this as an excuse to hold off on having a conversation for too long. Effective feedback can still occur over video or phone. I recommend using the channel with the least interruptions. If you know that a video call will likely have a bad internet connection, then a phone call is much better—you'd rather not be 'frozen' partway through the conversation. Of course, it is much easier to read body language and check emotional responses in a face-to-face conversation, especially in comparison to written feedback, which should only be used as a last resort or to reinforce what has been said in a discussion after the meeting.

Do not stockpile feedback. If you wait weeks, or even worse, until the annual performance review, it will be overwhelming for the person receiving it. It will feel like drinking from a fire hose, and they will most likely go into fight, flight or freeze as they will feel under attack. To avoid this, feedback should be given regularly.

Also, consider the state of mind of someone with whom you are planning to have a conversation. If the person seems stressed, wait until a time when they seem calmer and in control.

Frequent

We want our teams to have a continuous improvement mindset. We can do this by creating a culture where feedback, both positive and constructive, is normalised, regular and frequent.

There should be no surprises in an annual performance review and delivering feedback frequently should avoid this. People fear performance reviews if they have not had any indication about their performance throughout the year.

In Stephen Covey's *Seven Habits of Highly Effective People*, he uses the metaphor of an Emotional Bank Account—five deposits for one withdrawal. Finding the right balance of positive and constructive feedback is essential. A general rule of thumb is that for every constructive piece of feedback, you need to give five pieces of positive feedback. This doesn't mean that in the actual interaction, you're giving five pieces of positive feedback and then one negative piece of feedback. It means that over time, *consistently acknowledge* when others are doing things right—rather than just *thinking* it.

As we mentioned earlier, your feelings and beliefs about giving positive feedback may impact your willingness to provide it. If we practise this five-to-one ratio, when we give constructive feedback, others are more likely to take it on board because you've built rapport with them, and they trust you.

What is your Emotional Bank Account ratio for feedback with individuals in your team?

Positive intentions

If you want to give feedback because you want to blow off steam, get something off your chest, show that you are right, show that another person is wrong, or bring someone down because you are angry or frustrated, then you are *not* ready to be giving feedback.

If you want someone to learn and grow from the feedback or want to understand their perspective, ensure your intentions are coming from a positive place first. When you have a positive mindset, you feel more comfortable about providing feedback.

Focus on behaviour

When you give feedback, focus on the behaviour rather than the person or their personality traits. It's not that the person is lazy. It may be that they don't have the specific skills required to do what you have asked or don't fully understand the impact of their behaviour.

Avoid making assumptions and interpreting the situation on their behalf. Instead, give them something tangible by focusing on the specific situation and behaviour that was observed. For example, 'When you arrive ten minutes late for every meeting, it makes me feel like you don't value and prioritise the team'. This is a specific behaviour that has been observed.

Be mindful of how you share your internal thoughts, as it can completely change the dynamic of a conversation.

Interactive

Feedback conversations need to be two-way and interactive. It shouldn't be a case of you talking at them. Instead, you should make it clear that you want their input, their perspective of the situation and their skin in the game. It is important that the person feels they have a voice and they are being heard. Give them the opportunity to share their perception of the situation and try putting yourself in their shoes. For example, ask a clarifying question during the feedback conversation such as, 'What's your perception of the situation?'

Being curious is a critical skill for a thriving leader. In *Difficult Conversations* (2011), the authors discuss that asking questions with the goal of learning, paraphrasing their response so they feel heard and acknowledging how they may be feeling shifts the conversation into a problem-solving discussion.

Get the balance right

Radical Candor is a feedback model developed by Kim Scott (*Radical Candor*, 2019). When Radical Candor exists, we 'care personally' and 'challenge directly' the person to whom we are providing feedback.

Caring personally means treating people as humans and understanding that we are all people with feelings beyond our output at work. It's also about acting in service of people and contributing to improving their ability. It's taking the time to check in—are they okay? How are they progressing? Caring personally builds trust.

Challenging directly means having a fact-based discussion, saying what needs to be said and not stepping over issues. It is about sharing and playing back the behaviours that have been observed and having crucial conversations.

Radical Candor is like a compass. You can use it to gauge what type of feedback conversation you are having and whether you might need to dial up or down caring personally and challenging directly. Ask yourself, 'Am I caring a bit too much or am I not caring enough?' And likewise, 'Am I being a bit too soft or challenging a bit too hard?' You can adjust your approach in the moment based on how your feedback is being received.

Kim says that Radical Candor is like telling someone they have spinach in their teeth. If you have spinach in your teeth, you want to know. After all, you're the only person who can do something about it. Would you want to know if you had spinach in your teeth?

What not to do when giving feedback

When giving feedback, it's important to remember that it's not about you, your feelings and your viewpoint. Before launching into a conversation, consider the other person's feelings and opinions. Here are a few suggestions on what *not* to do.

Don't exaggerate

When describing situations, keep it fact-based. Using phrases like 'You always ...' or 'You never ...' will side-track your conversation. The frequency is less relevant; it is more about the specific situation. Focus on the behaviour or action you want them to stop or start.

Don't make it personal

If you open feedback with, 'Don't take this personally' or 'Don't take this the wrong way', guess what will happen—they will do just that.

Stay away from challenging integrity. Words such as 'unprofessional' or 'wrong' describe your viewpoint on someone's behaviour. Avoid expressing anything that sounds judgemental. Hold back from using these words as they are likely to make someone defensive. If you describe their behaviour in ways that threaten their core sense of self, they are more likely to shift from the issue to defend their character. Note that the exception to the rule here would be illegal behaviour.

Please, no feedback sandwiches

The feedback sandwich is where you deliver positive feedback, then constructive feedback, and then hide it with more positive feedback. This approach should be a thing of the past. As humans, we focus on negatives in feedback conversations and the positive message gets lost. Another problem is that when we give too much information at once, it can be a lot to digest and a lot for someone to take on.

It's not always clear-cut

Giving feedback is not black and white. Try to avoid using subjective language like 'clearly' and 'obviously' as this is absolute and can sound condescending, which is not helpful. You may be right, but it implies opposing views are wrong and the recipient may find the feedback insulting. People see things differently and that's okay but don't expect your viewpoint to be the same as others.

Feedback models

Thriving Feedback Model

Preparation is key. Think about what you want to say in terms of the feedback that needs to be given. Using a feedback model can help capture your thoughts so your feedback is fact-based and specific. This will help the individual to take action. If your feedback is specific, fact-based and supportive, the recipient is less likely to feel under attack.

The feedback model has been adapted from several research-based models and my experience working with thriving leaders. The model can be used for positive and constructive feedback. It is actionable and offers learning opportunities based on recommendations. Positive feedback is still a learning opportunity. Perhaps you want someone to apply their work in a different context or share the information with others.

Let's go through the model in more detail.

Step 1: Set the scene

Share intent and ask for permission

Before you launch into feedback, share your intent so the recipient doesn't jump to conclusions. People become defensive about why you are saying something rather than what you are saying. Being clear about why you are sharing feedback will help to alleviate this and it will put them at ease. We spoke earlier about having a positive intent, for example, you want the person to learn and grow—this is now about sharing that intent so they understand your purpose.

In *Daring Greatly*, Brené Brown talks about knowing that you are ready to give feedback when you are ready to sit next to, rather than across from the recipient—when you are willing to put the problem in front of you rather than between you. For me, I interpret this as getting your intentions right and sharing this with the person you are giving the feedback to.

Creating psychological safety is a key accountability of a thriving leader. Asking for permission is one way to create psychological safety when giving feedback. This may also be known as the 'micro-yes'. Before giving feedback, make sure they feel psychologically safe to receive it. Control is central to psychological safety, so if the recipient says it is okay, it gives them control. When you feel in control, you are more likely to feel comfortable, safe and that you belong. Most importantly, you will be more open to receiving feedback.

However, just saying, 'Can I give you some feedback?' may raise anxiety levels for some people. Be specific when sharing intent and asking for permission. For example, 'I'd love to discuss our client meeting. Is now a good time to catch up?' Asking for permission gives the recipient the opportunity to say yes or no or to pose a different meeting time. If they are not ready or are not in an emotional state to receive the feedback, they can still maintain control over *when* the conversation happens.

Some examples of sharing your intent and asking for permission include:

- I wanted to chat as I'd like to understand how I can support you better. When would be a good time to discuss?
- I see an opportunity for you in how you prepare for client meetings. Is now a good time to share my thoughts?
- I have a few ideas about how you could have greater impact with the supplier. Let me know when you'd like to chat.
- I'd like to discuss how we can work together more effectively. Is now a good time?

Step 2: Delivery

Situation and behaviour

Feedback should be specific so you can have a fact-based discussion. Be prepared with real-life examples, so you have evidence to back up what you are saying. This may require speaking to others to gather information for more serious feedback. People often ask questions to understand the feedback you are giving, so having examples on hand will benefit the conversation.

Be specific about the situation and behaviour you are seeking to address. When sharing the situation and behaviour use phrases like:

- When you ...
- At the ...
- In the ...
- When this ...

Impact

By describing the impact, you are explaining the why for the individual. This allows them to have an appreciation of how this behaviour and situation has impacted others, whether that is other people, other processes or customers. Explaining to the person the impact of their behaviour or a situation is often the part that is missed when delivering feedback.

When you describe the impact of the behaviour or situation, you should use words such as 'I feel' as people cannot refute how you feel. Therefore, the feedback is less personal. However, I know that some people don't like talking about their feelings in professional settings, so this can easily be replaced with language such as 'I observed' or 'I noticed'.

At times as leaders, we will receive third-party feedback that we need to deliver to someone. You can use the words 'it made others feel ...' or 'others observed' or 'they noticed' when you have not experienced the behaviour or situation yourself.

Some sentence starters when sharing the impact include:

- It made me feel ...
- I observed ...
- I noticed ...
- It was observed that ...

Pause

This is where a pause can be useful. It allows the person receiving the feedback to process what is being said. Holding some space for this and slowing the conversation will help them not to react. It can be as simple as counting to three in your head.

Step 3: Get buy-in and action

Clarifying question

Asking a clarifying question starts a two-way conversation, so you can understand their perception of the situation and how that landed for them. You might take a coaching approach for the rest of the conversation.

An example could be:

- What's your perception of the situation?
- What is your understanding?
- How do you think it went?
- What would you do differently next time?

Recommendation

The final element to feedback is actionable learning or a way forward. This can result from your clarifying question. Otherwise, you can make a recommendation like, 'I'd like to see you ...' It's about learning from the situation, taking action and being solution focused. It is often more effective when the recipient decides this for themselves. Taking a coaching approach allows them to create a solution based on the feedback. For example, 'What could you do differently next time?'

A thriving leader will have prepared solutions for cases where the recipient can't find a solution themselves. Some example sentence starters for recommendations:

- I would like you to ...
- I would love to see you ...
- I would recommend you ...
- In the future, I would recommend that you ...

Accountability and feedback

Finally, create next steps and expectations and identify how you will measure success. Be clear on how you will support the individual. Ask, 'What support might you need to do that?'

The individual should articulate their next steps. This allows them to take ownership. Ask, 'Based on our conversation today, what are your next steps?' or 'Where to from here?' (We will talk about this more in Chapter 4.) You can also gain their commitment by asking them to send you a written list of their next steps.

The Thriving Feedback Model in action

Once you have prepared what you want to say, find a trusted person who will listen as you do a run-through. Or practise the conversation out loud to yourself somewhere private.

STEP 1. SET THE SCENE

To create a safe space before sharing your feedback you need to:

- Share your intent
- Ask for permission

STEP 2. DELIVERY

Prepare fact-based information

- Specific situation and behaviour
- The impact of that behaviour

Pause (for 3 seconds)

STEP 3. GET BUY-IN & ACTION

Determine a way-forward

- Ask a clarifying question
- Recommendation for what the person could do differently next time or continue doing

Examples using the Thriving Feedback Model

Positive feedback example

'Can I have a chat with you about your presentation? I'd love to share with you the positive impact you had on the rest of the team.'

'When you identified such a creative solution and shared this approach with the team, it demonstrated to everyone that you can push boundaries with clients.'

'How did you come up with such a creative solution?'

'I would really love to see you continue to share your learnings on future projects. Well done.'

Constructive feedback example 1

'I wanted to check in with you regarding your email yesterday— just so we are on the same page. Is now a good time to chat?'

'I've noticed you have a real strength for identifying problems, which you did in your email. At times, it makes me feel like you don't want to be part of solving the problem. I'd love for you to come to me with solutions when you identify an issue.'

'So, how do you think you could approach this differently?'

'That's a great idea. I also understand that you have already tried a few different strategies before coming to me. Next time, let's set up a time to work through this together. This will allow you time to think through a few possible solutions. How does that sound?'

Constructive feedback example 2

'Is now a good time to catch up, as I'd like to talk to you about our recent project and how we can work most effectively together?'

'When you checked in on my progress several times a day, it made me feel like you didn't trust me to complete the project and I couldn't maintain my focus on the task.'

'How do you think we should check in with each other on our next project?'

'I would like it if we agreed on specific milestones and check-in points to ensure the project will be completed on time.'

Difficult discussions

Difficult discussions will always be ... well ... difficult. Preparation is key. The unexpected will always happen, but the more prepared you are the better the conversation will be. Plus, the more you can prepare for a difficult discussion, the more likely it will be successful. Stephen Covey's second habit is 'begin with the end in mind'. The principle is that all things are created twice. First mentally and then physically.

We all know that humans are unpredictable and that things don't always go to plan, so it is important to pre-empt what may not go to plan or derail the conversation. That way, you can prepare a response. Below are some questions to consider before having a difficult discussion. I suggest using this list and the feedback model to be fully prepared for the conversation. The time investment upfront will result in a better conversation and, therefore, save you time in the long run.

Begin with the end in mind:

- Do I need to have a discussion?
- What is the critical challenge or issue?
- What is the key message or outcome I want?
- How are my feelings impacting the situation?
- What do I want them to think, feel and/or do after the discussion?

During the discussion:

- How will I open the discussion?
- What key messages will I convey?
- What may derail the discussion?
- How will I keep it on track?
- How will I manage my emotions?

Before the discussion:

- How will I position the discussion?
- What do I need to do to prepare?
- What evidence or examples do I need?
- Who do I need to speak to?
- What mindset do I need to be in for the discussion?

Creating a culture of feedback

A strong feedback culture values and encourages feedback—leaders listen to employees and feedback is considered and acted upon. Importantly, there is consistent, clear communication back to team members about why or why not feedback was or wasn't acted upon. Let them know when you make a decision or change based on someone's feedback. This is positive reinforcement and encourages the individual to continue to give feedback. Lead with vulnerability; strong leaders show a willingness to receive and learn from feedback. Be transparent about where leadership can improve. Organisations with feedback cultures invest in their employees and encourage individual, team and organisational growth.

Create feedback standards and consistently role model and communicate what they look like. A challenge for leaders is finding the best way to let their teams know they are doing a great job or where they need improvement. Recognition and celebrating success is important and often forgotten.

Encouraging a feedback culture is the best way to address performance issues and acknowledge the hard work of the team and individuals. Innovative and agile organisations are often more willing to look for improvements. However, this doesn't mean they are equipped to provide and accept feedback within their teams.

To support a feedback culture, you must provide training and resources to your teams for giving *and* receiving feedback. Most training focuses on how to give feedback; however, receiving feedback is equally, if not more, important. Nurturing a feedback culture relies on having a safe environment where employees are willing to give honest feedback without ramifications.

Creating a feedback culture requires planning, so here are a few ideas to get you started.

- Create psychological safety so there is a safe environment for feedback.
- Role model receiving feedback by asking for it.
- Find the right balance of positive and constructive feedback and provide outlets for employees to give and receive both regularly.
- Feedback cultures can be achieved through feedback training, reward and recognition, employee surveys and 360 reviews.
- People with a growth mindset believe their abilities can be developed through dedication, learning and hard work. Strong feedback cultures value this mindset as you are continually learning and growing. (We will talk about this more shortly.)

When leaders and organisations incorporate feedback into their culture, it increases engagement, retention, productivity and motivation. Employee recognition increases retention and productivity: 69% of employees say they would work harder if they felt their efforts were being recognised through feedback and 66% of employees would leave their job if they didn't feel appreciated.

As thriving leaders, we need to create a culture of feedback, celebrate success, listen to our team members and take action to make the workplace we lead better than when we arrived.

How do you feel about listening to, understanding and then taking action from feedback? Consider the positive impacts of listening to and acting on feedback in Kate's story in Chapter 2.

Receiving feedback

We all have a role to play in terms of the culture of feedback in our organisations. Thriving leaders know how to receive feedback. In *Thanks for the Feedback,* Stone and Heen discuss that as the receiver, you control the reaction and whether the feedback is understood, accepted or adopted. That is where behavioural change can begin.

It's interesting how some conversations stick with you for life. The simplest piece of advice can change something in your approach. What feedback have you had that has really stuck with you? Why was that feedback so memorable?

I remember a time when I worked with John Cox, now CIO at Coles. We were going through an interview process at the time I was the People & Culture Partner and he led a large division within technology. We were meeting with different candidates and afterwards we would debrief privately to discuss our thoughts on each candidate. I had given some very direct comments on one specific candidate and after my delivery to him, I backpedalled quickly to soften my message as I had perceived my delivery as harsh. John, in this moment, gave me some important feedback. He said, 'What you said was valuable. Instead of sharing that direct comment, regretting it and editing your comments, you could take a moment to process the feedback on that candidate. Pause. And soften the message upfront on your delivery. This way you will have more impact with your comment'.

So why was this feedback so effective? For me, it was delivered in a way that helped me learn a new skill. It was tangible and practical, and I could understand it easily. I also trusted the person giving me the feedback and saw him as credible.

Now think about feedback that did not land well for you. I don't want to drudge up any demons, but when I ask this question in my courses, I'm told it was personal, not actionable, not delivered well, there was nothing to learn from the feedback, it wasn't specific, it was contradictory and unclear.

Triggers when receiving feedback

What happens when we receive feedback?

When we receive feedback that we think is critical, it causes tension. As humans, we want to learn and grow, but we also want to belong and feel respected and accepted. Sometimes we feel pulled in opposite directions because we are triggered in different ways.

Stone and Heen discuss three triggers we experience when we are receiving feedback. First there is the truth trigger. When we receive feedback and we feel the feedback is not factual, it will elicit a truth trigger and we'll probably question the feedback. In those situations, ask for examples so you can understand, and share your perspective of the situation. Do this constructively; however, there is no need to defend your position.

The second is a relationship trigger. This depends on the relationship we hold with the person giving us the feedback. The stronger the relationship, the more likely we are to take it on board. If we think the person giving us feedback doesn't have our back or we don't think they're credible, we're less likely to take that feedback on board. In some cases, that feedback could still be helpful to us, so test that feedback with someone you trust or with whom you have a strong relationship.

The third is the identity trigger. When we receive critical feedback, it is normal to question ourselves or go into a negative spiral about our self-worth. We must remind ourselves that the feedback is to do with our behaviour and a specific situation. It's not about you as a person.

Can you identify with these triggers?

Abraham Maslow talks about human motivation in his hierarchy of needs model. The model is based on neuroscience research that implies a certain five social domains activate the same threat and reward responses in our brain that we rely on for physical survival. We are commonly motivated to fulfil basic needs before moving on to more advanced needs as we move up the pyramid.

When we receive critical feedback, we often think it's impacting a higher-order psychological need such as esteem; however, it's probably more of a safety need in terms of us needing to belong and having a sense of security when we feel socially threatened. When you are receiving feedback, consider how it may be impacting you.

Understanding our mindset in terms of the threats we might

experience when receiving feedback is important. How do you take feedback on board? How are your behaviours perceived by others?

Tips for receiving feedback

Stay curious

Carol Dweck wrote the book *Mindset* to describe the way people think about ability and talent. She believes that fixed and growth mindsets exist on a continuum. A fixed mindset suggests your abilities are innate and unchangeable. You see failure as permanent and are more likely to view critical feedback as a personal attack. With a growth mindset, you view your abilities as something you can improve through practice. You see failure as a chance to learn and you are focused on the journey to improve.

> *'In a growth mindset, challenges are exciting rather than threatening. So rather than thinking, "oh, I'm going to reveal my weaknesses," you say, "wow, here's a chance to grow."'*
> —Carol Dweck

We can have fixed mindsets about some things and growth mindsets about others. The good news is that you can develop a growth mindset. It's important to have a growth mindset when we are receiving feedback. It forces us to look at the feedback as a learning opportunity and to stay curious.

When receiving feedback, come from a place of curiosity, ask questions and seek to understand. Asking questions or asking for examples will help you to truly understand the feedback.

Hold boundaries

Hold boundaries when receiving feedback. If someone wants to offer feedback but you're about to walk into an important meeting, say, 'Look, now is not a good time. Is it okay if we catch up later today or tomorrow?' Or if the conversation has started and you're feeling emotional (and you know you aren't going to get your emotions under control), pause the conversation and have it later. You are in control of your own psychological safety: understand how you are feeling in the context of what is happening and hold those boundaries.

Some people who ask for feedback are really seeking validation. If we are asking for or receiving feedback but what we want is validation, we are not likely looking to learn and grow. Prepare by opening your ears and your mind to the feedback.

Manage emotions

Manage your emotional reactions. When our amygdala is hijacked, we react and respond emotionally as the neural pathways have bypassed the prefrontal cortex—the logical part of our brain. Here are three ways to manage your emotional reactions:

1. Count to six in your head before you respond. This is the time it takes for the chemicals that are released during the amygdala hijack to disperse.
2. Focus on your breathing. Slow it down into a rhythmic pattern using box breathing. Breathe in for four seconds,

hold for four seconds, breathe out for four seconds, and hold for four seconds.

3. Do a math problem in your head. This activates your prefrontal cortex, the logical part of the brain, so you are less likely to react emotionally. The distraction helps to reduce the emotional response.

Determine what action you will take

Feedback is a gift so take it on board. Taking on constructive feedback gracefully is a skill. No one likes to hear what they are doing wrong, but we all need to hear it so we can learn and grow. After receiving feedback, create a plan as to how you will apply it and take action. Your immediate action may be reflecting on the feedback.

Asking for feedback

Show that you can take it! Role model receiving feedback. Invite feedback through the whole organisation. Ask for feedback.

> 'We can't just sit back and wait for feedback
> to be offered, particularly when we're in a
> leadership role. If we want feedback to take root
> in the culture, we need to explicitly ask for it.'
> —Ed Batista

But rather than asking a big question like, 'Do you have any feedback for me?' ask, 'What's one thing I could do to improve?'

Most people will be able to come up with something tangible that you can action easily.

Thank the person. It can be uncomfortable giving feedback. Even if you don't agree with the feedback, thank the person and agree on the next steps. The *first* next step for you might be taking time to digest the feedback.

Some people are feedback junkies. I once worked with a General Manager who always asked for feedback. It got to a point where I didn't have any more feedback to give. Sometimes, you don't have feedback to give and that is okay.

Summary

Thriving leaders create feedback cultures as they lead to high performance. Often, reframing a difficult conversation to a feedback conversation can change our perception of the type of conversation we want to have.

People prefer to receive feedback that matches their personal style. It is important to tailor your feedback to the individual and the context.

Find the right balance of positive and constructive feedback and provide outlets for employees to give and receive both on a regular basis. Approach any difficult conversation as a partner or collaborator. This shows that you are working together and have the intent to reach a win-win outcome for all. In building a growth mindset culture in your organisation, you'll always be looking for ways to improve, learn and grow.

📝 Actions

- Self-reflection: What feedback has had the greatest impact on you? Why did it have such a profound impact?
- Self-reflection: Where have you 'challenged directly' or 'cared personally' a little bit too much? What was the outcome?
- Use the Thriving Feedback Model for your next feedback conversation. Use the QR code below for a template. Each time you have one of these conversations, assess how you went. What went well? What is one thing that could be improved? This will assist you to continue to learn and grow.
- Use the difficult discussion questions ahead of your next tough conversation. Use the QR code below for a template.
- Ask your team, 'What is one thing I could do to improve?'

https://www.thrivingculture.com.au/tlbook

CHAPTER 4

Coaching

*'Coaching is about raising levels of
awareness and responsibility.'*
—Sir John Whitmore

What is coaching?

Thriving leaders coach their team members. Coaching is a structured conversation where you challenge and support an individual to learn, grow and maximise their potential. Coaching builds self-awareness, and drives action and accountability. It helps build skills and improve performance.

There are many definitions of coaching, and they all hold a similar premise. The International Coaching Federation defines coaching as 'partnering with clients in a thought-provoking and creative process that inspires them to maximise their personal and professional potential'.

Coaching is an approach to learning and development that is centred around the learner. It is a great way to clarify purpose and values and set meaningful goals. Coaching focuses on asking questions, actively listening and holding space for the other person. It involves setting goals and understanding what the team member is experiencing and thinking. It also explores options, challenges new thinking and gains commitment to action.

Most people naturally like to help others solve their problems. In fact, it is quite likely that you moved into a leadership position because you were a great problem solver and a superstar at delivery. When you move into a leadership position, you need to help your team members so they can solve problems for themselves. This is a fundamental shift for leaders. It is challenging to move from providing guidance and advice to asking questions and trusting that the individual has the answers. This skill requires you to let go and shift from being directive to empowering your team member to own the outcome.

Types of coaching

The term 'coach' gets thrown around a lot. There are many types of coaches, so it is important to delineate some key differences.

An executive coach works with individuals one on one to achieve specific coaching goals that support them in identifying and fulfilling their potential at work and in life. There are also specialist coaches such as leadership, sales, business, performance and career coaches. As the name suggests, these coaches specialise in a field, for example, a leadership coach provides coaching to people who wish to develop their leadership capabilities. These coaches are predominantly external, although some larger organisations invest in internal specialist coaches.

This book is focused on the leader as a coach. The critical difference is that when you are coaching as a leader, you have positional power and are part of the organisational system. Hence, you have a different level of vested interest in the outcome compared to other specialist coaches. External coaches are not part of the system so they can be more impartial in their approach.

As you read through this chapter, I encourage you to consider how you can apply these skills to coach yourself. We all instinctively self-coach to some extent. Some people are more intentional with this, and others have created reflective practices to help them learn. You can apply some of the models and tools to coach yourself on challenges you want to overcome or write down your responses to coaching questions.

In addition, you may apply these learnings to peers. Peer coaching can be invaluable, so don't feel this is limited only to your direct reports. If you are a parent, you may wish to apply some of the techniques with your children.

The power of coaching

I can remember when I truly understood the power of coaching. I'd had a career that spanned many People & Culture roles as an individual contributor. When I started working for Drago Mitkov, it was only my second leadership role.

Drago was an influential and empowering leader who was both personable and driven. To set the scene, I was going into my end-of-year performance review. Luckily, he regularly offered feedback throughout the year so I knew there would be no surprises.

What made this meeting so memorable was that he asked powerful questions and took a coaching approach to the conversation. When he asked questions, I gave myself the positive and constructive feedback I needed. His feedback reinforced what I said.

He provided strong direction about where we wanted to head next, but space and empowerment so I could guide the way to reach that outcome. I felt energised, empowered and I had clarity.

Personally, this was one of the most significant shifts for me. After experiencing a powerful coaching experience, I knew I wanted to take the same approach with my team. I enrolled in a coaching course and immediately saw the shift in my conversations with my team members. I thought I had already been coaching because I was great at asking questions; however, they were mainly closed or leading questions. They were suggestions or advice disguised as questions.

By taking a coaching approach with my team, I watched them step up in their roles. They were more empowered, and it was rewarding to see them flourish.

What approach do you take when you meet with your team members? Are you always directive or do you ask questions?

Benefits of taking a coaching approach

The International Coaching Federation (2009) states multiple benefits to coaching: 80% of people who receive coaching reported increased self-confidence and over 70% benefitted from improved work performance, relationships and more effective communication skills.

Learning and skill development

Coaching helps develop the skills and capabilities of our team members. It allows them to reflect so they learn. The transfer of this new skill, knowledge or way of working translates into stronger performance at an individual and team level.

In *Tao of Coaching*, Max Landsberg discusses how coaching benefits you as the leader and the person you are coaching. It increases your effectiveness as a leader by helping others develop and grow. There is a benefit to both parties. In the *Coaching Habit*, Michael Bungay Stanier highlights that the daily habit of coaching empowers you and team members and allows you to refocus and clarify your purpose. The mutual benefits are clear.

Builds confidence

Coaching helps your team members build confidence in their abilities. It is an excellent way to identify strengths and focus on these to help solve challenges they may be experiencing. Encouraging your team members to keep track of their successes and accomplishments builds confidence and awareness of strengths.

As a coach, you will often need to challenge your team members' limiting beliefs. Creating a psychologically safe environment where feedback is embedded into the culture allows team members to experiment and fail because they understand that failure is a learning experience. This builds confidence and empowers them to step up and have a go.

In their 2014 study, Gyllensten and Palmer demonstrated that an increase in confidence due to coaching led to better job performance. The areas that they highlighted were creatively solving problems, applying knowledge and assertively tackling challenges. This also benefitted them outside work as they reported having happier relationships at home and being less likely to bring work home.

To coach effectively, I encourage you to explore strengths, challenge limiting beliefs and give people a safe place where they are heard and understood.

Frees up your time

Leaders often believe they don't have time to coach. Yes, there is a time investment at the beginning, but you save time in the long run when your team members are self-sufficient and solving their own problems. It's a long-term game that you're playing. Give a man a fish; he'll eat for a day. Teach a man to fish; he'll eat for a lifetime.

Landsberg suggests that 'many great coaches believe that investing 10 minutes in coaching teammates will generate 20 minutes of extra time per day'. You can delegate more to your team when you take a coaching approach, which frees up more time for you to focus on what you want.

Would you like more time in your day?

Drives solutions

Coaching shifts the focus from a problem-based conversation to a strengths-based, solution-focused discussion. In a coaching conversation, you will reflect on the past but then look to the future to devise a solution.

When we are always problem-focused, we can play the blame game. It is essential to identify the problem you are trying to solve so you and your team member know you are solving the right issue. Use the past as a context point to understand the root cause, then move to a future-focused approach where you can influence the situation and drive progress towards a solution.

What ratio of meetings with your team are problem-focused versus solution-focused?

Coaching empowers your team to solve problems for themselves and drives action. When coaching, a key role is holding your team members accountable for what they committed to doing after the coaching session. This helps them take ownership.

Improved relationships

Taking a coaching approach builds the relationship you have with your team. It shows that you believe they have the answers and that you trust them to come up with their own solution. In addition, when you listen to others, they feel heard and valued— this strengthens and improves relationships.

How to coach

Asking rather than telling

In the past, the prevalent leadership style was 'command and control'. This meant directing and micromanaging situations. In recent years, the pendulum flung the other way, and a coaching and empathetic leadership approach was deemed more effective. In reality, there is a time and place to be more directive, offer advice and make suggestions. Such situations include when you are inspiring your team around your strategy and vision, when you are training your team or offering advice on a technical piece of work. If you do this all the time, you may be perceived as trying to control the outcome or micromanaging the situation.

You need to interpret and understand when it is appropriate. Is it a learning opportunity where the individual can create their own solution? If yes, then a coaching approach is the preferred style you want to use. When we ask questions, it feels empowering to the person on the receiving end. When we play the role of coach, counsellor or mediator, we often *ask* more than we *tell*. It feels controlling when we tell people what to do.

In Chapter 1, we discussed the different roles and expectations of a thriving leader. We are likely to be telling when we are the visionary or when we are offering advice and training. When we mentor and manage, we are telling and asking. When we counsel, mediate or coach, we are asking and listening.

You need to build rapport with the person you are coaching. Ways to build rapport with your team can include using collaborative and supportive language such as 'we' and 'our'. Our body language is also a powerful predictor of mood and relationships. Ensure you have a neutral stance and open body language. Nodding your head is also a useful technique. The relationship you have with your team members will be reflected in your coaching discussion, so notice this in terms of your language, body language and being present.

Closed versus open questions

A closed question is a question that elicits a 'yes' or 'no' response or can be answered with one to a few words. When we ask closed questions, we are 'closing' our thinking.

Examples of closed questions:

- Are ...? Are you going to contact the client?
- Can ...? Can you come into the office?
- Do ...? Do you have the report?
- Will ...? Will you update the presentation?
- Did ...? Did you speak to their manager?
- Have ...? Have you tried this?

When we use closed questions, we are often making assumptions and leading people a certain way—perhaps the way we think the conversation needs to go or to the solution we believe is best.

Open questions are more expansive in nature. By asking open questions, we generate new thinking, deepen reflection and insights, and truly understand. It is also a great way to determine how committed someone is to the conversation and the outcome. Of course, you *can* use closed questions but use them sparingly and for the purpose of clarifying your understanding. For example, 'Just so I understand, did you mean X?'

Examples of open questions:

- What ...? What is the best approach?
- How ...? How could you overcome that?
- Why ...? Why do you think they responded like that?
- Where ...? Where would you like this to go?
- When ...? When will that happen?
- Which ...? Which option will you take?
- Who ...? Who can support you?
- Tell ...? Tell me more about your approach?
- Describe ...? Describe how that made you feel?

'Why' is an open question. We need to be aware of our tone when asking a why question. People are likely to become defensive when you ask a 'why' question. Often, it is better to reframe the question into a 'what' or 'how' question. For example, 'Why did you do that?' can sound like you are judging them. A better question to ask is, 'What made you take that approach?' You are still asking the same thing but in a curious and less judgemental way.

We naturally ask a mixture of open and closed questions. Some people tend to ask more closed or leading questions than others. I was guilty of this before I started my coaching journey. I recommend adding more 'what' and 'how' questions into your everyday interactions with your team and seeing how the conversations shift.

What ratio of open to closed questions do you ask of individuals in your team?

Funnel questions

When we have an effective coaching conversation, we go deeper than the surface understanding. The funnel approach to asking questions starts by asking a broad question, then a clarifying question and then a probing question. You start broad and funnel your way in. You get more specific the deeper you get into the conversation.

Example of a funnel approach:

- Broad question: How did your presentation go?
- Clarifying question: What do you mean by not so well?
- Probing question: What specifically was the feedback?

Starting with open questions allows space for the person to share what is most important to them, rather than what we think is most important.

Active listening

Active listening is the ability to be completely present. This means not being distracted or preparing your response or next question. It requires you to listen deeply. Other than asking questions, the key fundamental skill needed to be a good coach is to actively listen.

What is happening when we listen? Our brains are busy. In fact, the human body sends 11 million pieces of information per second to the brain for processing, yet the conscious mind can only process 50 bits per second (Britannica.com). Filters assist our brain to process this information. Our beliefs, values, assumptions, biases and interpretations also impact our ability to listen. In *Conversational Intelligence*, Judith Glasser states that research shows we, 'drop out of conversations every twelve to eighteen seconds to process what people are saying; we often remember what we think about what another person is saying because that is a stronger internal process and chemical signal. In other words, our internal listening and dialogue trumps the other person's speech'.

Distractions are our most significant barrier to listening. Listening starts with you. Mental distractions can be thoughts about what you will have for dinner, remembering that you need to pick up the dry cleaning or that you forgot to send that email to your boss. Then there are physical distractions like checking your phone, noises in the office and alerts on your computer.

We are constantly bombarded with distractions. This only makes listening harder. We need to actively remove as many distractions as possible so we can be fully present. Ensure your phone is on silent and face down on the table, and that your computer isn't in direct sight. If you are on a video call, quit and close your emails and any instant messaging.

Four levels of listening

1. Pretending to listen: Not being present, being passive when listening. The old nod and smile.
2. Selective listening: Listening out for specifics based on what's on your mind or of interest to you. This means only listening to certain parts rather than the whole.
3. Listening to respond: Listening purely to formulate a

response. In this scenario, we are only half listening as we are too busy planning our response.

4. Listening to learn: Listening to understand, being attentive and empathetic and focusing deeply on what is being said. You digest before you start your response. This is a holistic approach.

You know when you're actively listening because you'll start using the language your team member is using. This means you are absorbing what they're saying.

Being present, concentrating and actively listening takes practice. And between you and me, it's exhausting because you are focused on the other person and less so on yourself. In regular conversations, you'd expect that each person would speak 50 per cent of the time. In a coaching conversation, the 80/20 rule should apply—80 per cent of the time listening and 20 per cent of the time talking. This is an excellent ratio to keep in mind when coaching your team to ensure you are listening actively more than talking. Also, when you slow your natural pace, it creates more space to listen.

When we actively listen, we also focus and interpret the emotion of what is being said. In doing this, we make meaning of the words being spoken. For example, 'You seem frustrated, excited, concerned'. What is said and what is meant can be two different things. In his book, *Deep Listening*, Oscar Trimboli shares that 'We speak at 125 words per minute but listen to 400 words per minute'. Our brains are processing what we hear faster than someone speaks. This means we can get distracted easily, but it also gives us the opportunity to make meaning from what someone says.

Finally, playing back what you hear is powerful, 'So what I'm hearing is ...'

The power of silence

It is fair to say that I like to chat. When I learned the power of silence and what it created, it changed how I coached. I learned to be comfortable with silence. Most of us like to fill awkward silences because the empty space feels uncomfortable. However, filling that space is more about you than it is about the other person; it is your discomfort.

One of the many nuggets of gold I learned at the Institute of Executive Coaching and Leadership (IECL) was Why Am I Talking? (WAIT). When you ask a coaching question, allow space and quiet time for the recipient to think about and construct their reply. Just breathe, and in your head ask, WAIT—Why Am I Talking? For others, counting (slowly) to five is helpful. It not only helps you achieve the 80/20 rule, but you will notice that when people have space to think, they will generally continue discussing what is important to them.

When you start coaching (and if you are anything like I was), you will be so focused on preparing your next question that you stop listening to what the person is saying. I learned that it is far better to actively listen to what is being said, pause to think about your next question and then ask it. Often the other person will have more to say, so give yourself time to think about the next question.

Another technique I was guilty of on my learning journey to becoming a coach was asking double-barrelled questions. This is when you ask one question and then ask another question on top of it. I believe there are two reasons we do this. First, we have not thought through our question fully, so the first question isn't necessarily the question we wanted to ask; therefore, to clarify, we add another question. Second, to avoid the uncomfortable silence, we decide to fill the space with an additional question. Keep your questions clean and ask one at a time. Otherwise, it can become confusing for the team member being asked the question(s).

We want to avoid over-complicating the question. This also shows up when we decide to add context ahead of our question so the other person knows you've understood what they're talking about. Again, this can cloud your question. Keep context succinct and ask clean questions.

Avoid solving their problem

You've moved into your role because you're an awesome problem-solver and great at your job— isn't that why you were promoted to lead a team?

We tend to solve their problems rather than supporting and empowering them to solve them for themselves. We feel we already know the answer or have the right solution or we have made our minds up as to what we think is the best way forward. You should hold your solutions lightly and be curious and open to other perspectives. Slow down and allow space for the individual to devise the solution. I know this will feel uncomfortable to start with.

When we solve our team's challenges, we usually operate in the 'rescuer' dimension of the drama triangle (Karpman). This is where we try to be the hero. This enables victim behaviours or a sense of helplessness in team members who always need rescuing. We want to empower our teams to solve their own problems.

Reframing problems into opportunities

When someone comes to you with a problem and they are using a lot of negative talk about what's happening, try to reframe it by taking a strengths-based approach. Reframe their challenge into an opportunity by leveraging their strengths. Ask a question like, 'Which of your strengths could you draw on to solve this problem?'

Coaching models

The GROW Model

The GROW Model was created by Sir John Whitmore and his colleagues in the late 1980s and over the years, it has become the most popular model for coaching for leaders. GROW stands for Goal, Reality, Option and Way forward.

Goal

Clarity and aspirations: Agree topic for coaching and what they want to achieve.

The goal is to agree on the topic for discussion and what you want to achieve from the coaching conversation. It may be a longer-term aspiration, or it could be a short goal that a team member needs to work through immediately. You may want to explore meaning. Someone might say, 'Today, I really want to talk about my work/life balance'. So, you might say, 'Okay, what does work/life balance mean to you?' This helps to clarify meaning and joint understanding.

You want to agree on specific objectives, so you are clear that you are focusing on the right thing.

Reality

Awareness including obstacles: Examine the current situation in terms of the coaching goal.

Reality is understanding the current situation and unpacking the key elements and relevant information. This allows the coachee to understand the facts of the situation from their perspective. It is best to ask lots of what, where, when and who questions when you are in reality. What's happening for them? What are others saying about the situation? Who else is relevant? What are they saying? When did they realise this was a problem?

Get them to share how they have approached the situation so far.

Options

Identify and explore all possible solutions: Solution-focused utilising strengths and resources.

The options section allows team members to think more broadly and deeply about how they can solve their challenge. Remember that they may be feeling stuck in terms of how to approach the situation. Often the first thing we come up with might not be the best solution, so it's about the power of brainstorming ideas and stretching people beyond their habitual thinking. A great question to repeat is, 'What else?'

Once they are clear on a few options, weigh them up to understand which idea they want to progress with.

Way forward

Actions and accountability: Identify the actions that will be taken and by when.

The way forward is confirming their next steps. What will they do and what actions will they take? This is the opportunity to explore what may get in the way and how they will overcome that. It allows for you, as their leader, to hold them accountable to their actions outside of the coaching conversation.

You want your team members to create clear next steps and identify how they will measure success. These accountability measures should come from your team members. Ask them to email you their list of next steps as a way for them to take ownership.

Please note that the W in GROW is sometimes called Will or Wrap up. I like Way Forward as it demonstrates the actions and accountability you want the team to take.

> *'We learn more from people who*
> *challenge our thought process than*
> *those who affirm our conclusions.'*
> —Adam Grant

Example GROW questions

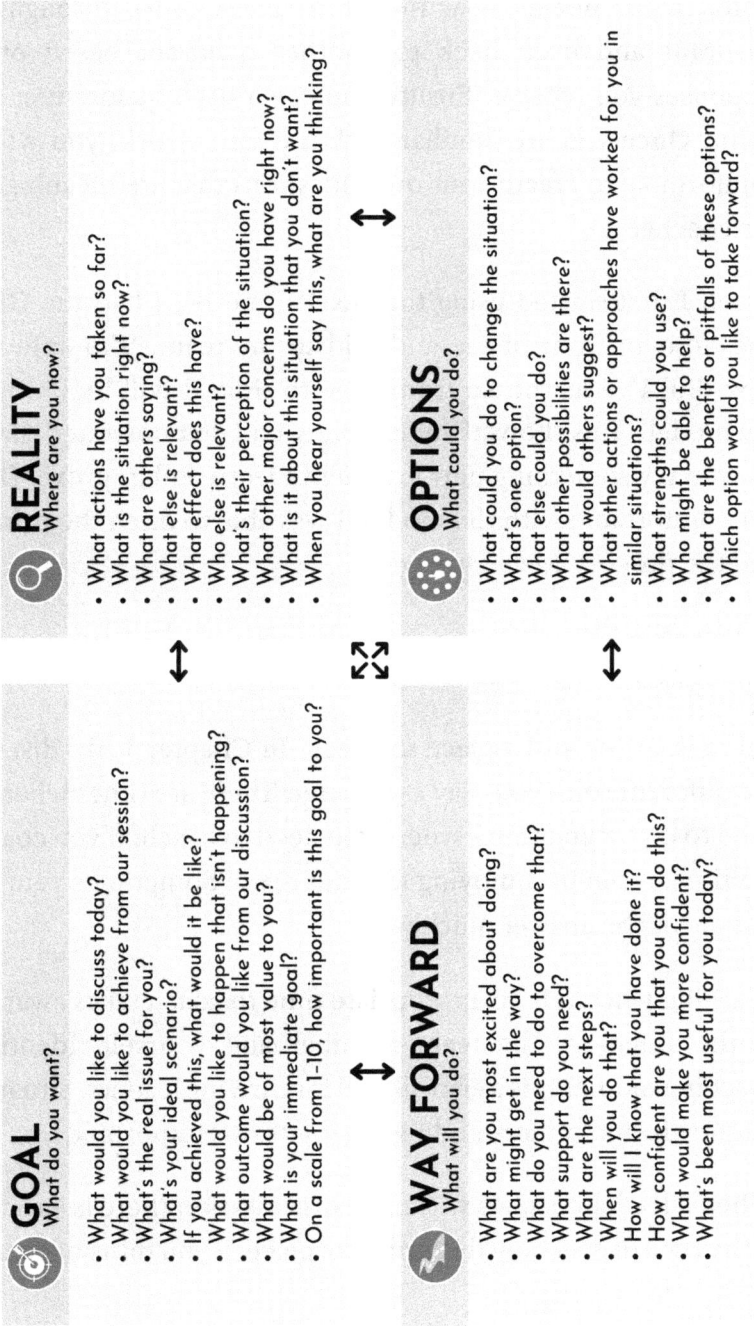

GOAL
What do you want?

- What would you like to discuss today?
- What would you like to achieve from our session?
- What's the real issue for you?
- What's your ideal scenario?
- If you achieved this, what would it be like?
- What would you like to happen that isn't happening?
- What outcome would you like from our discussion?
- What would be of most value to you?
- What is your immediate goal?
- On a scale from 1-10, how important is this goal to you?

REALITY
Where are you now?

- What actions have you taken so far?
- What is the situation right now?
- What are others saying?
- What else is relevant?
- What effect does this have?
- Who else is relevant?
- What's their perception of the situation?
- What other major concerns do you have right now?
- What is it about this situation that you don't want?
- When you hear yourself say this, what are you thinking?

OPTIONS
What could you do?

- What could you do to change the situation?
- What's one option?
- What else could you do?
- What other possibilities are there?
- What would others suggest?
- What other actions or approaches have worked for you in similar situations?
- What strengths could you use?
- Who might be able to help?
- What are the benefits or pitfalls of these options?
- Which option would you like to take forward?

WAY FORWARD
What will you do?

- What are you most excited about doing?
- What might get in the way?
- What do you need to do to overcome that?
- What support do you need?
- What are the next steps?
- When will you do that?
- How will I know that you have done it?
- How confident are you that you can do this?
- What would make you more confident?
- What's been most useful for you today?

Note, this is not a linear model. You will move through each quadrant and even back to another quadrant based on the responses you receive. Ensure you cover each quadrant at some point. Once you are familiar with the framework, you will feel comfortable to create your own questions that are meaningful to the coachee.

When I first started using the GROW model, I had the GROW questions in front of me and said to my team, 'I'm applying a new skill I've learnt, so from time to time, I will look down at the model'. This showed vulnerability and demonstrated that it is okay to try something new in order to learn and improve. Once I felt comfortable with the model, I was able to ditch the printout, and the process flowed freely.

When to coach

There is a time and a place to coach. In Chapter 1, we discussed the different roles you play as a leader. There are times where you need to direct and times where you need to coach. If you coach all the time, it can be annoying for your team. Sometimes your team just needs the answer quickly.

Learning when it is an appropriate time to coach takes awareness of the situation, the team member and yourself. Identifying coaching moments is a critical skill for thriving leaders. Situational leadership and understanding the context is important.

When a leader coaches within an organisation there is variability in the type of coaching that will take place. If you think of coaching as a continuum, one end is informal and the other end is formal and in-depth using GROW.

Informal:

- Question-rich conversations (2–5 minutes)
- In-the-moment coaching opportunity (3–5 minutes)

Formal:

- Coaching conversations (5–20 minutes)
- Formal coaching (20 minutes–1.5 hours)

Anderson (2013) discusses that most leaders' coaching experiences lie at the informal end of the coaching continuum.

In-the-moment coaching

These are corridor conversations or when someone approaches your desk with a question. Rather than solving their problem, try asking four simple questions so that they can come up with the solution themselves.

When you are coaching in the moment, start with a Reality question—because by the time someone comes to you, they are already in this quadrant. Next ask a Goal question, an Options question and finally, a Way Forward question.

This could look like:

Reality: What's on your mind?
Goal: What's your ideal scenario?
Options: What's one thing you can do?
Way Forward: When will that happen?

Reality: What's up?
Goal: What do you want instead?
Options: What can you do?
Way Forward: What's your next step?

Reality: What's going on?
Goal: What outcome would you like?
Options: What possibilities are there?
Way Forward: When will you do that?

Create a version in your own language. Having these four simple questions in your back pocket will ensure you are prepared to support your team to think for themselves.

Coaching for performance

When we coach for performance, we focus on tangible objectives that help individuals deliver the expectations of their role as best as possible. It is results- and job-oriented and can centre on feedback or take place in more formal performance meetings.

Taking a coaching approach when having a difficult conversation shifts the discussion from telling to asking powerful questions so the individual can identify the issue. Often, when you start a difficult conversation by asking questions, the recipient may bring up the issue on their own, but this is not always the case.

Coaching for development

When we coach for development we focus on the skills, capability, knowledge or learning opportunities for an individual. It can also centre on feedback and can take place during a career conversation or formal development planning conversation. The focus is primarily on professional development and career aspirations.

I encourage you to use these tips and take a coaching approach when coaching for performance, development or giving feedback.

- Ask open questions.
- Use the GROW Model.
- Really listen to what is being said and understand their perspective.
- Have an attitude of discovery and curiosity.
- Let the individual feel heard and understood.

Skill vs will

To coach effectively you need to hold the belief that the individual holds the answers within. You are there to support and facilitate ongoing learning. If you don't feel that they have the answers within, consider taking a training or mentoring approach to bridge any capability gaps.

You can use the Skill Will Matrix created by Hersey and Blanchard to assess the capability and motivation of a team member. This model refers to skill in terms of level of capability, and will in terms of attitude and motivation. Where someone sits on the matrix will impact how and if you will coach them.

If a team member has low skill and low will, the best approach is to manage, direct and train. This requires regular check-ins to provide feedback and being available to provide advice. You also want to understand what drives and motivates the team member so that you can connect their values and drivers to the work they do and to the organisation's values.

When an employee has low will and high skill, you need to focus on their motivation. A visionary or mentor approach can be useful to connect them to purpose and their why. Determine how you can play to their strengths and the things that matter the most. Ask them what it would take for them to feel motivated with the work they do each day.

When a team member has high will and low skill, the approach is to guide them. This is where you can train them, buddy them up, get them to shadow others and instruct them. Provide praise and positive recognition when the skill is demonstrated and allow them the safety, if appropriate, to do so. Let them fail fast and learn from their mistakes.

Finally, when a team member has high will and high skill, you will want to stretch them so they continue to learn and grow. Delegate tasks of greater complexity, allow them to take accountability for outcomes and be more involved in making decisions. Take a coaching approach to empower them.

Creating a coaching culture

A coaching culture is a learning culture. Coaching cultures encourage experimentation and the development of new ways of thinking and doing in an action-orientated and accountable environment. Coaching is a powerful way for organisations to achieve their goals. Google's Project Oxygen is an ongoing strategic initiative to identify what it takes to be a great leader. Being a good coach is the number one skill that leaders needed to demonstrate to be a successful leader.

Gone are the days when the leader in the business is the smartest person in the room. Leaders can quickly access information from people within their organisation by asking powerful questions. This also empowers team members to step up and be confident.

How do you create a culture whereby leaders coach their teams so they can come up with their own solutions to their own problems?

- Articulate the benefits of coaching so it is widely understood in your organisation.
- Train all leaders in your organisation so they have the capability to coach.
- Once trained, create coaching circles so leaders can practise their skills with the added benefit of being coached.
- Advise leaders to take a coaching approach when managing performance and development conversations. Consistency and building regular operating rhythms mean coaching is more likely to be embedded.
- Role model and coach your team.

The International Coaching Federation (ICF) in partnership with the Human Capital Institute (HCI) completed research in benchmarking strong coaching cultures within organisations. They discovered the top three ways coaching supported organisations' goals and strategies were leadership development (55%), talent development (51%) and performance management conversations (49%). This further supports the fact that coaching cultures help people develop.

Summary

Coaching clarifies purpose, values and goals. It helps individuals to understand the facts of a situation and explore options. Coaching should help an individual articulate their commitments.

Coaching is a way to develop your team members. It builds confidence, frees up your time, and drives solutions and action. The biggest shift for leaders when they coach is moving from being directive to asking questions. It can be challenging not to solve problems for your team. When leaders coach, they need to be solution-focused and help their teams gain clarity and work through solutions. By using techniques like asking open questions, actively listening and allowing space through silence, a thriving leader can build the coaching muscle.

There is a time and place to coach. Using your situational awareness, you can gauge if coaching is the right tool to use in that moment. It is a powerful tool in performance, career and development conversations.

Take a coaching approach when facing difficult conversations and providing feedback. Difficult conversations, feedback and coaching are all skills that must be practised. Have a mindset of curiosity when you coach.

Create a coaching culture within your organisation.

📝 Actions

- Over the next week, monitor the number of open versus closed questions you ask your team.
- Reframe closed or leading questions into 'what' or 'how' questions.
- Use the GROW model with a team member. Use the QR code below for the GROW model. This could be a coaching for performance or development discussion.
- Create your own in-the-moment coaching questions—four simple questions. Use the QR code below for a template.
- Consider how you will create a coaching culture within your team or organisation.

https://www.thrivingculture.com.au/tlbook

PART 3

Connect to purpose

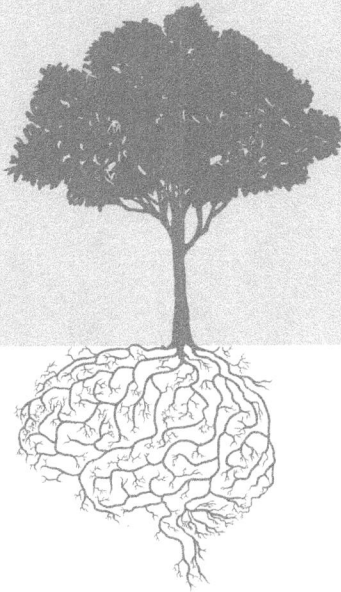

When writing this in 2022, we have just come out of over two years of COVID-19 pandemic. Leaders all over the world have been adapting to hybrid work, and this dynamic will continue to evolve. Whilst hybrid teams are not a new concept, we are still learning how to best support our teams and adapt to different ways of working. Research reported that during the transition to remote work, the 'watercooler' chats were the moments most missed. These social, relationship-building activities allowed spontaneous moments of social connection during the day, keeping managers across what's going on and building trust and morale between teams.

Ultimately, regardless of how your teams work, we want them to feel engaged, productive and happy at work. This means we need to be purposeful in the way that we connect with our teams, hold them accountable and communicate. These are simple steps to create an inclusive environment.

CHAPTER 5

Accountability

'The only way we succeed as a group is not simply following directions, but in keeping each other accountable for our actions.'
—A.J. Darkholme

What is accountability?

Accountability is about providing clarity for your team. Accountability is delivering on a commitment, using initiative to follow through and taking responsibility for an outcome.It eliminates ambiguity, creates boundaries and ownership, and provides clarity for moving forward. Accountability involves understanding what is required in terms of quality and timeframes. This should feel empowering because someone is trusting your skills, knowledge and experience. It is a privilege.

Holding team members accountable and setting goals through clear communication is a skill that many leaders find challenging. When we delay having important conversations, problems escalate and accountability isn't addressed. (Use the tools from Chapter 3 to help with this.)

A thriving leader must build their confidence and comfort level if they want to be high performing.

There is a balance between your individual accountability and the accountability you must hold of your team. You need to deliver on your own commitments and have ultimate accountability for the team you lead. So, it is your responsibility to ensure that you and your team are clear on why, what, who and when deliverables or tasks need to be met. You will not be successful unless your people are.

Accountability doesn't mean you can't be compassionate. Remember the leadership dial from Chapter 1? You need to balance being assertive and empathetic. Accountability is delivering on a commitment to actions and understanding what may be getting in the way for your team member achieving what is expected. Some of this may be outside of their control, which means you must combine compassion with accountability.

Lack of accountability

Where there is a lack of accountability, there are excuses— individuals deflect from issues and there is a lack of follow-up or follow-through. People feel overwhelmed and stressed and begin judging others to protect themselves.

While it is tempting to look to others when there is a lack of accountability, it is more likely the outcome of another issue. Most of these issues sit with you as the leader, so you first need to diagnose what is driving the lack of accountability so that you can address it.

Ask yourself the following questions:

- Did I set clear expectations about the outcome?
- Were the expectations realistic?
- Do they have the skills to perform the task?
- Have I communicated why this is important?
- Have I provided support?

Barriers to holding others accountable

Sometimes it just feels easier to do things yourself. It can be less stressful than calling people out when they haven't followed through on a commitment. In a recent clture.io survey, 93% of those surveyed said they were unable to align their work or take accountability for desired results. One-third felt their priorities frequently changed, which created confusion.

When the goal posts continually shift, it is hard to hold your team members accountable as there is confusion about what needs to be delivered. Perhaps you haven't taken the time to think through roles and responsibilities or have only thought about it and not put pen to paper and clarified this with individuals. Maybe you lack clarity yourself about what needs to be done.

If priorities have changed, you need to clarify the new expectations.

You may fear upsetting someone if you hold them accountable. We want to be liked by our team and being assertive could affect our relationships. But we don't need to be liked by our people, we need to be respected. We need strong interpersonal relationships if we are to delegate accountability to others. It requires trust and a deep level of communication.

Wanting to be liked

A GM in a business felt uncomfortable being assertive with expectations. The team had worked together for ten years, and they knew each other well—perhaps a bit too well. He didn't want to be seen as dominant and he wanted to be liked. So when things weren't done as he had expected, he did the work for the team. This enabled a victim/rescuer dynamic within the team, and it unintentionally told the team it was okay not to meet expectations.

Some leaders don't want to micromanage their teams, so they are given free rein, which leads to ambiguity and a lack of follow-through. This leads to frustration as the team member hasn't delivered what was expected. However, if the goals are unclear, the lines of accountability become blurred and this behaviour is reinforced. This can also paint a picture to the rest of the team that underperformance or letting others down is okay.

If any of these barriers apply to you, you are not alone. A recent CEO Benchmarking Report found that 18% of CEOs find holding people accountable their biggest weakness.

How to hold others accountable

Accountability is about creating clarity, which you can do by following these four steps. I refer to these as the 4Cs to Accountability.

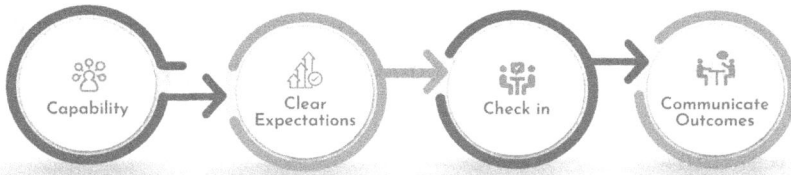

Capability

Assess capability

Assess who is most suitable to complete the task. A good leader understands their team members' strengths, skills and experience. They recognise individual growth opportunities. When determining who is most suitable, assess whether they have the capability to perform the piece of work. Set them up for success by asking these questions:

- What are the skills and strengths of this team member?
- Who has the capacity and the skill set to complete the deliverables?
- What skills do they need to deliver on expectations?

Upskill where required

Provide support, resources, training or tools so they can succeed. How can they acquire the skills if they do not have what's necessary? Build a plan to support them. This can be through knowledge transfer with another team member, shadowing someone or having a buddy they can rely on when they get stuck. Ensure that your team member has the capability or the potential to develop the skills to deliver what you expect of them. Otherwise, you will be bitterly disappointed, and nobody will be happy.

Delegation

The shift from doing the task to leading others to complete the task takes skill. There are many benefits to delegating, but many managers still fail to delegate effectively. Delegation is only effective if you hold your team accountable.

Leaders can often spread themselves thin due to being under-resourced or lacking the trust to hand over the reins to their team. Delegation can be challenging for various reasons. You may feel that you will do a better job or that it will get done quicker if you do it. You may not feel comfortable letting go of control, or you may be unsure if your team member can do the task.

All this may also be true at first but delegating helps to teach team members new skills and capabilities; it allows them to step up and this empowers them. It also gives you back time, helps improve team productivity and builds a culture of trust and learning.

Being able to delegate is a crucial skill for a thriving leader.

Consider the following when working out what work to assign to a team member:

- Which deliverables would be a good learning experience for them?
- Does this play to their strengths?

- Are they capable of delivering on expectations?
- What tasks don't play to your strengths or leave you lacking energy when you do them?

Clear expectations

People need to understand why they are doing a piece of work. You won't be able to hold someone accountable if it is unclear what you expect of them. This means being clear about the outcome and how you will measure the success of achieving that outcome.

Articulate the outcome

Too often, leaders share that they found it challenging to hold team members accountable as they hadn't set expectations. Clearly articulate the outcome. Explain why the deliverable is essential and what is required. Give clear instructions and expectations. Give them autonomy to own the task and authority to make decisions where appropriate. It may seem like an investment of time up front, but in the long run, it will result in more time for you to focus on the more strategic elements of your role.

Depending on the individual's capability, you may also provide guidance as to how they should achieve objectives. For more capable team members, it can be valuable to let them choose the pathway to achieve the best outcome. This will empower them to make decisions for themselves. This is not always possible and it depends on their level of capability. Your high-performing talent may have ideas about what needs to be achieved, and in these instances, you can co-create the important outcomes that are required. You must be active in this process so you know your team members are focused on the right things.

When meeting with a team member, ensure it is a collaborative process where both parties are actively engaged. Get them to summarise their understanding of what is being asked of them so you can be sure you are on the same page. This gains their buy-in and commitment to achieving the outcome. If they play back something different, it is an opportunity to reiterate and provide further clarification.

Measures of success

Sometimes we expect our team members to be mind-readers. Being clear about what success looks like and how you will measure it means everyone is on the same page. As a leader, it is frustrating when you expect one thing and get something different. But this can be avoided: determine the measures of success together. Some activities are not easily measurable and it is okay if the outcome is a qualitative measure.

Check in

When setting expectations up front, be clear on how and when you will check in. Having short meetings to check progress on milestones means the individual receives regular feedback on how they are tracking and you can brainstorm the most effective way forward.

Create an environment where people feel comfortable asking for help and support. Working as a team to solve issues in performance will encourage innovation and strengthen collaboration and trust. This can only happen with regular check-ins.

Accountability helps your team members take full ownership of their work. Checking in does not mean micromanagement. When you provide autonomy to your team but don't check in, they can lose sight of what is important, go off track, or get tied up in ambiguity. Give autonomy so they know they are trusted to deliver, but also be available to provide support when needed. To provide autonomy, you need to be confident in the knowledge, skills and experience of the person or people doing the work. Autonomy without check-ins leads to ambiguity.

When you micromanage your team, it often stems from your personal fears of being unable to deliver on expectations. This needs to be addressed if there is a capability issue within your team. When you micromanage, the team becomes frustrated as people feel restricted. Micromanagement becomes disempowering and people feel stressed and overwhelmed.

Micromanagement permeates

A large manufacturing business was led by a woman whose communication created fear and belittlement. When things weren't done to the leader's expectations, she would dive into the detail and micromanage the situation. The fear drove a blame culture that resulted in finger-pointing between teams about who was at fault. Team members were defensive; they protected themselves and were reluctant to make decisions.

How she led the leadership team impacted how they led their teams. It also affected the organisation's culture. The micromanagement permeated through the organisation, and everyone was doing the jobs of the layer below them. When the leader was replaced, the leadership team had to relearn how to make decisions for themselves, hold their teams accountable and empower them.

Feedback

Review the work and provide positive or constructive feedback so people can learn and improve.

Provide clear feedback on their progress against goals and understand the barriers and obstacles to achieving expectations.

When holding team members accountable, create a culture where feedback is regular and ongoing. If you have clear expectations and measures of success, the feedback can be fact-based, specific and actionable. Be clear whether the individual is delivering on expectations or not as this will help people know where they stand. (Refer to Chapter 3.)

Cadence

Ensure your one-on-one meetings, team meetings and reporting requirements consistently reinforce the accountability of individuals and the team to meet goals. Agree on specific milestones and check-in points so that team members can ask questions and you can provide feedback regularly. It is important to build this into your operating rhythm.

Communicate outcomes

When you hold your team members accountable, you must communicate outcomes so they know how they went delivering on expectations. Most people feel the word consequence is harsh because their brain automatically concedes a consequence to be negative. However, there needs to be a consequence or outcome for accountability to occur. Accountability needs to have consequences—positive or negative.

Three outcomes should be communicated depending on whether the team member met expectations: reinforce, redo and release.

Reinforce

Provide specific positive reinforcement when a team member nails what you asked of them. Let them know they have done an excellent job and what they did so well. Praise publicly, acknowledge their hard work, and over time, this could lead to them doing more complex work, moving into a role with greater complexity, a promotion or pay rise—all additional signs of positive reinforcement.

Redo

If the work is not up to your expectations, provide specific feedback and ask the individual to try again. There is a tendency, usually when time is of the essence, to do it for them. An example of this is reviewing a report for a team member rather than tracking changes and having a conversation about what they could have included or areas to improve. When you submit the report without the feedback loop, the same mistakes will appear on the next report. This can feel frustrating, but how were they to know what needed to be done differently?

Leaders who do the work for their team members end up overworked and burnt out. It is an essential step in the team member's learning process to redo work that is not up to standard.

Release

Poor performance needs to be addressed immediately. When it isn't, it indicates to the other team members that sub-par performance is acceptable. Consistently addressing under-performance builds trust in you and the team. There will be times when the person is not the right fit for the work; this may turn into a conversation about a role that is better suited and plays to their strengths, or you may need to let them go.

When a team member isn't performing, it is important to understand why. Have a conversation to understand what is going on for them. Be consistent when addressing under-performance within the team; it must align with the organisation's values and expectations of the role.

Known for quality and transparency

JVAT is a risk and assurance consultancy firm with offices in Melbourne, Brisbane, Adelaide, Sydney, Bristol (UK) and Boise, Idaho (USA). The business started in 2017 with an idea to change how risk and assurance is perceived—by shifting the paradigm from being an inhibitor to an enabler. To achieve this, JVAT provides complete solutions to clients by offering technical, enterprise risk and management consulting services, and its own products and training solutions.

In the first five years, JVAT expanded to more than 60 specialists worldwide. JVAT has delivered hundreds of projects and developed bespoke software solutions for multiple billion-dollar global corporations.

I spoke with Jimmy Stewart, Managing Director, on how they have created a high-performing accountability culture at JVAT.

When holding people accountable, be clear on expectations, understand the task and their capabilities and be clear on the level of quality you require of the task. It's about ongoing dialogue and communication and providing praise and recognition. It's about the interpersonal relationships. Relationships are born out of trust. However, trust and accountability are not the same things. Accountability and responsibility are interlinked. The feeling you get when you are responsible for something is on an emotional level: it is a psychological nudge that drives accountability within someone. If they can't do the job you have asked of them, then coach, mentor and check in. People focus on the task, but it is about the individual. They will have a good crack if they feel supported and are valued. That's empowerment.

It is more than a monitoring process. Set and forget doesn't work. You care about the outcome, so be available to clarify any questions. For me, it is about having a shared responsibility for an outcome. Delegation is a process that introduces people to what needs to be done so that they can take ownership. You need to tell a story when delegating. Like a jigsaw box, you need to describe the whole picture so they are clear on the outcome. You need to provide the context using clear communication so they understand what a good outcome looks like. People often miss the success criteria and it becomes abstract. As leaders, we need to remove uncertainty and create objectivity

> *around it—that is the key to delegation. It's about clarity and the quality of the outcome.*

To effectively hold someone accountable, you need to understand the direction the team is headed. You need a clear strategy, goals and operating rhythm that supports this.

Strategy

Strategy helps organisations set a direction that all team members can align to. A strategy articulates what makes your organisation unique and different and provides value. A strategy informs what areas to invest your time and money in, the organisation's structure, resource requirements and how you respond to market and stakeholder needs. Operationalising strategy is where the rubber hits the road.

The strategic pyramid explains the elements that help an organisation set a vision, determine the most important areas to focus on, and translate that strategy into an implementable plan. This can inform the organisation's plan on a page.

The *purpose* is a statement that articulates why the organisation exists. This statement should inspire people and express the change you want to see.

The *vision* is where the organisation is headed in the long term (3–10 years). The vision should be aspirational to team members.

Strategic priorities are the critical areas the organisation will focus on to achieve the vision.

To operationalise the strategy, you need to set goals and have a plan to achieve those goals. We will talk through this in more detail below in *Objectives and Key Results* (OKRs).

This is all underpinned by culture, *values* and shared beliefs that demonstrate the organisation's behaviours.

If you are a leader within an organisation, you should be clear on the organisational strategy and where it is headed. If not, make a point of finding out. Thriving leaders have a team strategy to ensure the activities and areas they are focusing on support the organisation achieving its strategy.

How is your team contributing towards the organisation's strategy?

Goal setting

Goals need to be aligned to the strategic direction of the business. This is the way to operationalise your strategy so that it gets implemented. Deciding on the most important goals that will enable the execution of the strategy is key, but it can also be challenging. When we are focusing on too many areas, it is hard to get anything done. A lot of the time, the power comes in things you are not doing, saying no to or deprioritising. The leader needs to guide the team and individuals to focus on the right things.

*'There are so many people working
so hard and achieving so little.'*
—Andy Grove

Introduce a goal-setting framework to measure success. This goes beyond your day-to-day responsibilities.

Team goals help everyone to be motivated towards a common target. It allows the team to collaborate and be innovative and it provides a clear direction of how their work contributes to something bigger. It helps to bridge the gap between their individual work and what the organisation is trying to achieve. It also provides transparency and visibility of what everyone is working on.

I like to use OKRs. It is a simple system that can be adapted to suit your organisation or team. You can make it work for your operating rhythm.

OKRs

OKRs stands for Objectives and Key Results. It is a goal-setting framework popularised by innovative, agile organisations such as Google. OKRs are qualitative 'Objectives' that have quantitative measures of success known as a 'Key Result'. OKRs are used to identify the outcomes and measures of success that would be most impactful to enable the strategy over time. OKRs provide clarity for progress towards organisational targets. OKRs are set, tracked and re-evaluated frequently, usually quarterly.

Again, it is about focusing on a few key objectives and doing these well. For each objective, you create 2–5 quantitative key results that demonstrate the achievement of that objective. Once you have set your OKRs, you will determine the initiatives you believe will help reach your objective.

Objective: What we want to achieve.

Key results: How are we going to measure our success?

Initiatives: What are we going to do to achieve it?

In John Doerr's book, *Measure What Matters*, he explores

aspirational OKRs as visionary goals where you are unlikely to reach the target—a 'moonshot'.

> Koala started using OKRs in the early days and this continued to evolve over time. Sandy shared.
>
>> We introduced OKRs in year two. We had multiple iterations of how we used and thought about OKRs, and although it was never perfect, it was a great way to communicate priorities and align teams to the mission. The OKR process was a great way for each team member to understand how their work fed into the overall objectives and how each role was important in the business's success.
>>
>> Earlier in the start-up phase, we set stretch OKRs and scored our results knowing that achieving 0.7 was still a success. In corporate business, the likelihood of hitting goals is very well understood and often linked to financial benefits for the goal setters themselves. This stagnates big businesses from being disruptive; it normalises mediocracy. In disruptive start-ups where you're operating in uncharted territories, no one really knows what you're capable of. At Koala, we aimed for the stars and celebrated when we reached the moon.
>>
>> We reviewed OKRs as a leadership team and challenged each other in that environment. We shared our wins and failures in town hall meetings, and we took ownership when we failed. Owning our failures modelled accountability to the team and further cultivated the safe environment we were trying to create.

Committed OKRs are achievable and realistic goals that you

intend on reaching. I believe you need a mix of aspirational and achievable OKRs, as people get demotivated when they don't hit targets.

In my experience, OKRs work best when they are set at an organisational level, as well as a team level. Each team creates OKRs that contribute towards the overall organisation's OKRs. This is quite different to the cascading balance scorecard approach, which is a top-down command and control approach to goal setting. OKRs foster collaboration, as the team has ownership and accountability to deliver.

Using OKRs ensures you implement and execute a clear, transparent and measurable strategy. OKRs is a framework, but it's also a learning process and mindset for your team to think about and measure the work they do. It is about moving away from a focus on output and moving towards a focus on outcomes.

Having one person manage the OKRs is a great place to start. This person will ensure everyone understands the OKRs and can hold them accountable to the OKRs they have defined. They will ensure everyone is properly trained, engaged and has ongoing support.

Setting Objectives

- Align them to strategic objectives that enable the organisation's vision.
- Ensure the objective is a qualitative statement.
- Use verbs that demonstrate actions and what will be different.

Creating your Key Results

- Make them outcome-based instead of output-based.
- Key Results are either activity-based, meaning you are implementing something, so they should start with a strong action verb (eg deliver, launch, build). Or values-based, measuring the outcome such as a Net Promoter Score or Employee Engagement Score.
- They need to be measurable. If you don't currently measure it, a key result should be to determine how you will measure it.
- Organisational key results can be broad. For teams, they should be more specific in terms of what they can influence and contribute towards.

Example OKRs

Objective: Outstanding customer experience
Key Result 1: Net Promoter Score (NPS) of 8.0 (this is a values-based OKR)
Key Result 2: Resolve 90% of customer support tickets within 24 hours within the next half
Key Result 3: Win two national customer awards by June 2023

Objective: Improve our products and services
Key Result 1: 100% deployment of technology automation program by December 2023
Key Result 2: Release two new products to market by December 2023

Key Result 3: <5% rework on quality assurance of service deliverables within the next quarter

Objective: Increase sales volume
Key Result 1: Create a sales pipeline of $1million in lead generation by June 2023
Key Result 2: 20% uplift in sales revenue by December 2023
Key Result 3: Increase number of closed deals by 25% by December 2023

The challenge with goal setting is keeping it front of mind: make goals obvious and build them into your operating rhythm. Link your team to the purpose of the work and ensure it is meaningful by continually making the link and their work visible.

What frameworks and tools do you use to help your team remain focused, aligned and engaged?

Jimmy shared JVAT's experience with OKRs.

We went on a journey of discovery and maturity with OKRs. Understanding why you are setting them is important. We created a vision and set OKRs that could be executed across a cross-functional team so we could understand how we all fit in. We didn't want to create a hierarchy—we wanted to honour our flat structure. We learnt that a few OKRs are better. We found that setting individual OKRs doesn't really work; they become a job description or KPIs. We found it most effective to set organisation and team OKRs to keep things current and dynamic.

> *We created and educated our teams on the OKR lifecycle. We created a four-monthly battle rhythm where we could derive, deploy, monitor and review. We also created a monthly status report to regularly check in and ensure we agreed and were aligned.*
>
> *This allows us to be prepared to drop something if we need to.*

If you use OKRs in your business or with your team, you need to make them work for you and the context.

Operating rhythm

An operating rhythm creates a repeatable cadence so team members know what to expect week in, week out. It creates certainty and removes ambiguity. Just like setting my alarm each morning to go to the gym: I don't have to think about whether I want to go because it becomes second nature. The purpose of having an operating rhythm is to be clear on what you need to collaborate on and when.

You need to hold yourself accountable to the operating rhythm you have agreed upon. You must prioritise this cadence to create certainty and demonstrate the importance you place on these activities. Structure and expectations are important for your team—especially in times of change.

Your operating rhythm is part of your culture. It should be meaningful and suit your context. Everyone should be clear about each element in your operating rhythm. You should also review to ensure it is continuing to work for everyone.

JVAT created the JVAT Day. It is based on the science and psychology of high-performing teams and promotes productivity and efficiency, so they work smarter, not harder. The JVAT Day consistently creates structure and focus so they can operate at their best.

JVAT has built this rhythm into every working day:

Prioritise: *This is when the team coordinates and communicates daily goals. Writing goals down has been scientifically proven to streamline your day and increase your effectiveness.*

Focus time: *The team uses this time to be efficient and effective without distraction. They do everything in their power to create a two- to three-hour window of Zen-like stillness each day where they preferably have only one thing to get done. Protect this time like your life depends on it.*

Meet: *The team uses this time to conduct short and snappy meetings bound to 20 minutes. This ensures they have defined outcomes that result in clear actions. If these aspects weren't included, it wasn't a meeting, it was just a chat.*

Eat: *Try not to eat at your desk, it's bad for keyboard hygiene. It's good to take breaks.*

Creative time: *Let your creative juices flow: brainstorm, innovate and solve the unsolvable. It's all about ideas. Big or small, the key is letting yourself explore them. Innovate on old ideas or try to invent something new. Your only limit here is what you put on yourself.*

Organise: *It's almost time to finish up. Let's tick off those side tasks and plan for the next day to make your work as efficient as possible.*

Breaks: *Take them, it's important. Every 45 minutes, stand up, walk around and clear your brain. A five-minute break can inspire your next 45-minute surge and save you hours in the end. It's worth it.*

Meetings

Let's face it, some meetings can be boring. Make a commitment to me that you won't hold boring meetings. Get clear on the purpose of the meeting. What are you trying to achieve? Is it information sharing, collaborating, problem solving or decision-making? Who needs to be there? What's in it for them? What outcome are you looking for? The length, format and frequency are key. Then have some fun with it.

Ensure you are always meeting with purpose and are clear about the value for everyone involved.

Team meetings

Having a regular meeting rhythm with your team is important. This may be weekly, fortnightly or monthly. You should have a clear agenda. You will likely have operational meetings to discuss the day to day and strategic meetings that are less frequent, say monthly, bi-monthly or quarterly. You need to create space on the agenda in strategic meetings to innovate, create and problem solve with your team. This is often missed in meeting cadences. Work out the things you need to collaborate on and build this into your rhythm.

One-on-one meetings

You need to meet regularly with each person in your team. Whether that is weekly, fortnightly or monthly is up to you. Newer or less experienced team members may require a different cadence to more experienced team members. Some, depending on style, will want short and sharp meetings, where others may need longer. Again, it's not one size fits all.

Having regular one-on-one meetings stops the interruption cycle that happens within your day and creates boundaries. Did you know that it takes an average of 23 minutes and 15 seconds to get back to the task after a distraction? Show them what focus time looks like and set that example. Encourage them to establish focus time and set boundaries with other team members. Creating a balance between being approachable and available without being disruptive is important.

A one-to-one meeting shows your team member that you care as you are prioritising your most valuable resource—time. You should create a regular rhythm to discuss performance, their day-to-day work and how they deliver against expectations. This allows them time to ask questions and for you to provide feedback. On a quarterly or bi-annually basis, you should have a development meeting focused on the skills and capabilities they want or need to develop, career aspirations and a plan to get there. (Refer to Chapters 3 and 4 for skills to support these meetings.)

All-team meetings

These are sometimes called town halls or all-team briefings. They are meetings where everyone in the organisation, or business unit for larger companies, is exposed to key messages from senior leaders. The purpose is to keep everyone informed of what is happening in the business. Consider how you manage key messages with your team. (We will cover this in detail in Chapter 6.)

JVAT's operating rhythm has laser focus. Here is what Jimmy had to say.

Routine is good. People love it. It's about empowering people to do things their way. It's not about being micromanaged. People feel comfort with routine. It is stable and irrespective of how they are feeling. They know what is happening, especially during chaotic times like COVID. We have a clear battle rhythm at JVAT:

Weekly Executive Leadership Team (ELT) Brief where an ELT member communicates to the organisation so everyone understands what is going on.

Weekly Team Training Talk where a team member shares information on a topic for 15 minutes. These are recorded and we now have a library of over 200 trainings.

Two stand-up meetings per week for each team where teams discuss what is most important, planning, support, risks and blockers to their deliverables.

Senior Leadership Team weekly meeting that focuses on operations, and quarterly strategy meetings.

Weekly Reflections where every person in the organisation reflects and shares on their key learning for the week. This is also an opportunity to celebrate success.

> *Yearly Conference where all team members get together to understand strategy, celebrate success, have fun and build relationships as a team.*

Find an operating rhythm that will work for you and your team. Engage them in the process.

Transparency

Roles and responsibilities

It is fundamental that every person is clear about their role and responsibilities. Ideally, this should be in the form of a meaningful job description. This helps them to understand where they need to focus their time, what their job is and what it is not. Even if you work in a relatively small organisation, this is still important. If roles and responsibilities are not clearly laid out, it will result in duplication of work and things getting missed.

> *Sandy shared Koala's focus on accountability.*
>
> *We did a lot of work to focus on accountability at the 200-employee mark. If there is no accountability, there is no ownership and no risk so individuals will not apply themselves in the same way.*
>
> *We talked a lot about accountability as a leadership team and across the organisation. We became clearer in everyday work about who is responsible, by when and why. We focused on KPI metrics across teams separate to OKRs that represented BAU work.*

> *We linked how individuals were driving business and financial success. When individuals understand how their role drives success and how they can achieve results, it brings them comfort; they feel valued and they are ultimately more engaged.*

Visible work

Make the work visible by using workflow management tools. This shows who is accountable for what so team members can manage their workload and prioritise. This keeps the work visible to all, whether it is online or physical visual management.

It helps self-driven accountability as there is nothing better than peer pressure to incentivise people to work harder and meet their deliverables. People don't want to let others down. When reporting is visible and individuals self-report on progress to their peers, it helps to keep them on track. Autonomy gives people the responsibility to hold themselves accountable.

Ensure you have a conversation to understand why they didn't follow through. Getting under the hood of the issue means issues can be surfaced and worked through. When we get in a state of too busy, things go wrong or don't go to plan, and the *purpose* and the *why* are overtaken by the *what* and the *tactical*.

> *JVAT prides itself on the quality of its deliverables. They do this with a strong culture of accountability, transparency and visibility of work. They use a workflow and project management tool so everyone can see what everyone is working on, including clients. Distraction is*

minimised, and work is focused by having the JVAT Day and workflow management tools. Quality is their key criteria. Jimmy said.

Visibility and transparency are key to accountability. It's about conversations and creating a psychologically safe space to talk about what you are working on. Stand-up meetings with your team can help. We keep teams small—no more than seven people.

Decision-making

As thriving leaders, you need to make decisions that are in the best interest of your team and the organisation. Instil a culture where your team members feel equipped to make their own decisions, otherwise everything needs to come past you and this is time-consuming and disempowering. Office vibe's pulse survey showed that one in five employees do not feel they have enough freedom to decide how they do their work, and one in three employees do not feel they're appropriately involved in decisions that affect their work.

We talk a lot about empowering our teams but it is clear from the stats that only some have the power to act independently and make decisions.

What gets in the way of your team members making decisions?

Telling your employees that you trust their judgement and giving them the trust and power to make a call will build them up. If everyone understands their responsibilities and expectations, they should also know when they can make decisions on their own. Encourage them to find solutions to problems and only involve you, as the leader, as a last step.

> Take it a step further like Koala did and write down the beliefs to help inform decision-making at all organisational levels. When Koala had 20–50 employees, they could run really fast. When staff numbers grew above 50, the dynamic changed, and they needed to consider how to get the messages through the organisation in terms of how they think. Sandy shared.
>
> > If people can't make quick decisions themselves, they aren't able to work fast. This blocks them and slows down day-to-day tasks. Decentralising decision-making is hard, both as an organisation and as a leader. You must let go and focus your attention on giving your team the tools so they can make decisions in line with the company objectives. Our belief statement made it clear to our team what we believed and the reasons why. It created certainty.

As a leader, empowering your team to be confident with their decisions will set you up long term. However, you may feel uncomfortable making decisions yourself. Every day, we face hundreds of choices and we can suffer from decision-fatigue.

Here are a few simple strategies to help you if you struggle with making decisions:

- Try to take yourself out of the equation so your decision isn't driven solely by emotion.
- If you avoid making decisions, give yourself a deadline.
- Limit your choices and quantify the options.

- Use others for support and as a sounding board to help you feel more confident about your decision.
- Most importantly, be aware of the biases you hold as this will influence your decision-making.

Jimmy shared his thoughts on decision-making.

When I worked in the military, I was deployed into Afghanistan. The focus on that mission was intense. When there is a clear mission statement or a clear outcome for you and your team, you almost set the preconditions for the decision-making and accept it. How you do that is up to you. It's about using knowledge, skills, experience and assets. The extreme end of accountability is clear in the military—someone will die. This has an effect on your decision-making.

Decision-making is intrinsic and comes from thinking styles. Some people are critical thinkers and others are lateral thinkers. The danger comes when there is poor decision-making and you don't have transparency. I don't think there is a bad decision; the good or bad comes from who judges it. The optics of making decisions is a binary thing—good or bad. People are scared of the judgement that comes with making a decision. I'm confident in making decisions as I'm comfortable with uncertainty.

You need clear context to inform decision-making, and as the context changes you need to refine your decision.

A culture of accountability

To create a culture of accountability, it needs to be embedded in everything you do.

Reward and recognise when team members are being accountable and holding others accountable. Ensure you celebrate success. We often don't stop or slow down to enjoy our wins along the way as we are already onto the next thing. To motivate your team, it is essential to acknowledge and celebrate their successes.

Create rituals. When I was leading a team, I adopted a weekly ritual. Every Friday afternoon, I emailed my team (we were geographically dispersed) and shared three things I was most grateful for that week. Two of the things were work related and one was personal. The entire team responded with the things they were grateful for. As it was a large team, I ended up having to send my initial email on a Friday morning to allow time for the whole team to respond before the end of the day.

Share when you haven't achieved an OKR or have missed a deadline or goal, just like Koala did as a leadership team when they didn't hit their target. Likewise, adopt a reflective practice like JVAT, where they show vulnerability and share their learnings for the week. Shape the culture of accountability, so it suits your workplace culture.

JVAT prides itself on its culture of accountability.

We operate as a team; there is a sense of belonging, a shared vision and shared outcomes. There is an inherent trust that comes from that. We work hard on our high-performing team culture. It is reinforced daily. It's not just words; it is baked into the routine of how we work, and people see the results. The ultimate feedback is your client performance score. We delivered 207 projects and our client feedback score is 95%. This is how you know you are doing something right.

Summary

You must establish and maintain individual and organisational accountability measures that monitor team activities, assign responsibility and share the results transparently.

To hold your team members accountable, ensure each person has the capability or can be upskilled to do the task. Be clear on individual expectations and what success looks like. You can articulate the outcome but give team members space to choose the best journey to get them to the outcome.

Ensure you have regular feedback loops to check in on progress rather than waiting until the end of the deliverable. Communicate outcomes so team members know how they have performed.

Getting the team aligned with shared goals and creating a vision about where you are headed in the future is essential. Identify the strategic priorities that will support the vision. Operationalise your strategy using OKRs. You need to develop a plan on how you and your team will work together to achieve goals. Clearly and concisely articulate this plan. Reinforce these goals regularly. Have a clear operating rhythm and cadence that supports this. Don't forget to celebrate the successes.

▤ Actions

- Hold your team members accountable for applying the framework. Remember the 4Cs to Accountability: Capability, Clear expectations, Check in and Communicate outcomes.
- Set team OKRs and develop a cadence to review and align progress. Use the QR code below for an OKR template.
- Review or create an Operating Rhythm that works for you, your team and your culture.
- Write a list of ways to reward and recognise a positive accountability culture.

https://www.thrivingculture.com.au/tlbook

CHAPTER 6

Communication

'Leadership is a way of thinking, a way of acting and, most importantly, a way of communicating.'
—Simon Sinek

Everyone needs to be effective at communication—thriving leaders even more so. It is the most universal skill. Effective communication is how thriving leaders engage and inspire their people to follow them.

What is communication?

Communication is the ability to relay information in a simple, clear and meaningful way. It is a process of sharing and receiving information. To effectively communicate, you need a shared language and understanding of concepts. You draw meaning from sharing in all situations: face to face or using technology.

We communicate every day in many ways: verbal, written, body language and tone of voice. When we assign work, share information, provide feedback or coach, we communicate in some way. Thriving leaders are effective communicators; they have strong working relationships, high employee engagement and they support the organisation to operate productively.

Effective communication provides clarity, purpose and accountability. It encourages and demonstrates the culture within an organisation and needs to be role modelled by the leaders within it. A critical component of effective leadership is communicating clearly to different audiences with a consistent message. Communication involves active listening and letting people be seen and heard.

Barriers to effective communication

Poor communication occurs when there is a misunderstanding between what was communicated and how it was interpreted. There are many reasons why leaders fail to communicate effectively.

Style

A report from The Economist Intelligence Unit, 'Communication barriers in the modern workplace', found that the most frequently cited barrier was differences in communication style. In Chapter 1, we discussed the importance of understanding your own preferences and that of the people you work with. This is so you can adapt your style to the audience.

Not sharing information

When team members feel like they aren't hearing the whole picture, it leads to distrust. We know that trust is foundational to any high-performing team. When this isn't present, it will likely lead to team members making assumptions. You need to manage the narrative so workplace whispers don't do it for you.

Leaders are nine times more likely to be criticised for under-communicating than over-communicating (Flynn & Lide). Let your team know when you don't have the answer. Thriving leaders share relevant information and are transparent.

Information overload

This occurs when leaders overshare information or share information that isn't relevant or ready to be consumed. This leads to team members feeling overwhelmed and unsure as there is too much information. We are processing lots of information every day: emails, instant messaging, voicemails, phone calls. It's a lot! Thriving leaders filter information so that it is relevant to their team.

A General Manager within an organisation used verbose language to send essay-length emails to his team. When he would communicate expectations, his team was never clear on what he wanted as there was so much information. This caused a lot of ambiguity for the team that craved clear and simple communication. This resulted in the team not delivering to his expectations—but the expectations were not clear.

Not being heard

When communication is one-way, people feel like they are being spoken at. They feel like they don't have a voice and are not being listened to. They feel disrespected and undervalued. When they are interrupted, it demonstrates a lack of respect. Thriving leaders listen; they are approachable and they take on feedback (remember Kate from Chapter 2?). They check to see whether communications have been understood and if they haven't landed, they communicate in a different way so the team understands.

Assumed knowledge

We all experience the curse of knowledge where we assume that people know what we know. This cognitive bias has caused me to question what to include and not include in this book. When I facilitate and train, I am reminded that while something may be well known to me, it is new to others. Thriving leaders don't assume their team members know what they know—they communicate. This helps to inform their team.

Remote working and hybrid teams

It can be challenging to communicate effectively when some employees are in the office and others work remotely. This creates sub-cultures. Employees who work on different days have different experiences. This is heightened for those who work remotely as there is a tendency to favour the people who are more visible.

If you do have a mixed workforce, treat all employees as though they are remote. This way, you are communicating and collaborating equitably and are giving everyone access to the same information, people and tools so they can succeed regardless of where they are sitting.

Stress

Leaders cast a long shadow. When we are stressed and overwhelmed, it is noticed by those around us. This affects our ability to communicate clearly and calmly. Thriving leaders manage their emotions to avoid misunderstandings. Interestingly, the cause of the stress may be related to poor communication in the first place.

Tools

Not having appropriate tools or structure can cause leaders to not communicate effectively. There is no shortage of tools to communicate with your teams. You have access to video calls, email, instant messages, text and phone calls. The only barrier here is not being clear about what channel to use for what. There can be generational differences in communication preferences.

> JVAT use collaboration tools productively. They use an agile project management software to communicate between the team about the task and work being conducted throughout the business. They match the channel to the audience. Email is to be used sparingly. A conversation, whether face to face, via video or phone, is the preference. Email is for formal communications. Instant messaging channels are set up for teams to collaborate or direct chat for informal communications. Also, no communications are sent through focus time. There is a noticeable difference in their email culture as their days are not driven and dictated by hundreds of emails.

Impact of not having effective communication

There is a significant impact on leaders and organisations when employees don't communicate. David Grossman reported in his article *The Cost of Poor Communications* that a company with 100,000 employees loses on average $64.2 million each year due to inadequate communication and misunderstandings among employees. Knowledge workers in small- to medium-sized businesses cost those businesses on average $26,041 per employee for misaligned communications.

People leave organisations when there is poor communication, when change is communicated poorly and when there is a lack of direction from leaders. When there is poor communication, teams collaborate less effectively and have more workplace conflict. Poor communication leads to a bad customer experience. When communication is unclear, it can contribute to lowering employee engagement.

The Economist noted the most significant impacts of poor communication:

- 52% of employees said it leads to higher stress levels.
- 44% of employees reported that it causes failure in completing projects.
- 31% of employees said it causes them to miss their performance goals.
- 20% of employees in poorly communicative work environments said they experience obstacles in innovation.

Communication is a critical skill for a thriving leader.

How to communicate effectively

'Communication makes the world go round. It facilitates human connections, and allows us to learn, grow, and progress. It's not just about speaking or reading, but understanding what is being said – and in some cases what is not being said. Communication is the most important skill any leader can possess.'
—Richard Branson

There are many practical techniques you can put in place to communicate effectively.

Be clear and transparent

When a thriving leader communicates, they use clear and simple language. They inspire people through language that is easy to understand—everyone is on the same page. The vision and direction have been clearly articulated and understood by team members.

A thriving leader's message is transparent. They share what they can, and they acknowledge when they don't have the answers. They ensure what they communicate is timely so there is no uncertainty or ambiguity.

Avoid using acronyms and company jargon so that even new employees understand what is said. We appear more confident when we remove filler words like 'um', 'so' and 'like', as these reduce your credibility.

> Brookfarm is a premium gourmet food producer that is committed to regenerative agriculture. This family-run business focuses on producing consistent, high-quality products that centre around the environment and sustainability. I chatted with Will Brook, CEO at Brookfarm, about how he communicates effectively with his teams and connects them to purpose.
>
>> Authentic communication for us is about transparency first. You can inspire people without transparency, you can show them nice shiny things. But at Brookfarm, we offer a lot of trust and enough rope. We are transparent with what is happening in the entire business; we share our revenue, spending, margins, which products are better than others, what we might discontinue and new products.

Two-way communication

A thriving leader's communication is two-way; it is a conversation. It requires listening and taking on feedback as well as contributing perspective. When generative dialogue happens, challenges are solved and relationships are improved.

Thriving leaders take the time to understand whether messages have landed and they take on feedback from the audience when they haven't. They know that what they say may be interpreted differently from how they intended. This feedback loop is critical to ensure everyone involved is on the same page.

Will demonstrates two-way communication.

We had feedback from staff that we weren't doing enough around recognition. We listened, and once a month we celebrate staff birthdays. We stop, have cake and everyone sings really loudly. We use that time to recognise someone in the business for doing an amazing job and demonstrating the values. We now have a better cadence with this practice; it's a chance for connection.

Be inclusive

Thriving leaders make every single person feel important—even when communicating with a group. Where possible, engage team members in the conversation by asking rhetorical questions to get them thinking.

An effective way of doing this is by using collective language such as 'we', 'us' and 'together', rather than 'I'. This makes people feel included. Ensure you use gender, culturally and age-inclusive language. Using personalised language to the audience makes it easier for them to interpret your message. Make them feel important and show a genuine interest in them.

When I worked with Sarah White, now the Chief of Staff at NAB, I was always in awe of how special I'd feel after a meeting with her. I asked her one day, 'How do you make everyone feel so important?' She responded, 'I believe that everyone is important and if you have that mindset, then listening, respect and inclusivity follow, and your communication has greater impact'. This has always stuck with me.

How do you make your team members feel important when you communicate?

Tone of voice

Communication is more than the words you use. Your tone of voice is how you sound, the way you say things and the impression it leaves on others. It comes through when you speak and when you write. Your tone of voice influences how people listen to you and creates an environment where people feel comfortable. It should be authentic to you and portray the type of leader you are. Your tone of voice will change depending on the context of the message. You may need to sound confident and supportive for one message and authoritative and serious for another.

It is important to understand and use a tone of voice that is appropriate for the audience and the format of the communication. Does the communication need to be formal, informal or conversational?

In a study called, Surgeons' Tone of Voice: A Clue to Malpractice History, it was found that surgeons' tone of voice in routine visits was associated with malpractice claims history. They were assessed for warmth, hostility, dominance and anxiety. Those with higher dominance and lower concern and anxiety in their voice tones were significantly identified with previous malpractice claims compared with those who had no claims. This demonstrates that your tone of voice influences how you are perceived by others.

Thriving leaders are aware of their tone of voice and ensure it is appropriate and that it doesn't sound condescending or dominant.

Using pauses effectively and varying your pace is also an effective communication strategy.

Body language

Body language is all the non-verbal signals we portray when we communicate. Body language includes your posture, how you stand, how you move, your gestures, eye contact and your smile.

We make judgements based on body language and non-verbal expression. Your body language influences someone's first impression of you. People make up their minds quickly; some research suggests this happens within the first 2–3 seconds, others 7 seconds and 30 seconds. Whatever the number, people are quick to make assumptions about the type of person you are, your confidence levels and your status before a word has been spoken. Ensure you have a positive, open posture; make eye contact to build trust; and use gestures appropriately to emphasise points.

In Amy Cuddy's famous TED Talk, *Your Body Language May Shape Who You Are*, she introduces the power pose. She says, 'Our bodies change our minds, and our minds change our behaviour, and our behaviour changes our outcomes'. Before big meetings, job interviews or a presentation, find a quiet place to do the power pose process below. (I have found the toilet cubicle to be useful.)

- Stand tall and strong.
- Put your hands on your hips like superwoman.
- Next, put them up in the air and flex your muscles.
- Finally, raise them above your head like you've just won Olympic gold and you are doing a victory lap.

This will help you feel more assertive, confident and optimistic—with the premise that you will 'fake it until you become it'.

Smiling releases endorphins like dopamine and serotonin that put you in a good mood. Smiles are infectious. When you smile at someone, their brain automatically responds and they smile back.

Consider and observe your body language in different interactions. How can you make your body language portray the person you want to be?

Repetition

Repetition is vital for effective communication. We exponentially forget things we hear. People forget approximately 50% of new information within an hour, 70% within a day and 90% in a week. This is known as the forgetting curve (Ebbinghaus). This is all dependent on how complex the information was, how meaningful it was, how it was delivered and the wellbeing of the individual (including stress and sleep). Thriving leaders repeat messages even after they are bored hearing them.

> 'When you are tired of saying it,
> people are starting to hear it.'
> —Jeff Weiner

It is through repetition that we learn. Our brains create new neural pathways that are strengthened through repetition as we continually work to retain information. Consistency in messages provides certainty and clarity. To help you generate repetition and consistency, create stories and key messages that emphasise and communicate the message. Then repeat these over a variety of channels.

Understand your audience

To some, it may seem disingenuous, but every day we need to influence and persuade others to get work done. In the HBR article, *The Practical Art of Persuasion*, the authors suggest that to influence someone to change their mind, you need to ensure there is either logic (an argument that appeals rationally), emotion (consider your biases and heuristics and the emotion you want to elicit) or character (audiences' perceptions of you).

Thriving leaders tailor their messages to the audience to influence them. You must consider What's In It For Them (often called WIIFT) when preparing a communication. Ask yourself the following questions to frame the communication to your audience:

- Who is my audience? (eg demographics, expectations, knowledge or attitude)
- What motivates them?
- What are their three biggest challenges?
- What do I want my audience to think, feel or do as a result of my communication?

Based on your responses, what is the best way to communicate with them?

Learning styles

Understand your audience's style. People have different learning styles: visual, auditory and kinaesthetic. For visual learners, pair what you are saying with charts, diagrams or other visual cues. This doesn't mean images and videos. Auditory learners enjoy hearing words to understand concepts and they are also likely to verbalise their thought processes and enjoy talking things through.

Kinaesthetic learners apply their senses and experience to process information. They enjoy real things such as demonstrations, case studies and the practical application of the information. We all absorb information differently. Many people are multimodal, which means they use a combination of learning styles.

A multimodal approach can be useful to accommodate different styles. According to researcher and molecular biologist John Medina, if you 'hear a piece of information, three days later you'll remember 10% of it. Add a picture and you'll remember 65%'.

Approach

Consider the type of communication you are delivering to determine the best approach to communicate your message to your audience.

- Is your message formal or informal?
- Should it be written or verbal?
- Are you communicating to an individual, group, team or the company?
- Should the communication be one-way or two-way?
- How will the communication be reinforced?
- Is the communication confidential or sensitive?

Before presenting, practise, practise, practise. For verbal

communication, rehearse what you are going to say out loud several times. Then when presenting, make it conversational so each person in the room feels you are speaking directly to them. 'How might I do that?' you ask. Use the language your audience is using, relate to them in some way—ensure it is genuine. If you can, make it interactive. Get the audience to reflect on what they might do and an action they will take.

Thriving leaders adapt their communication style to complement their audience.

Will shares his communication style.

I've worked everywhere in the business since 2008. I understand people's roles, so I can show empathy for what they are experiencing. I don't adjust my communication style a lot. I see everyone as people, and I am interested in what they are doing. My concept is to treat everyone with the same level of respect. This is what I try to teach my kids—everyone matters. I will adjust my communication to the audience when it is technical. If the conversation is about machinery, I'll use operational style language. From feedback, in our business updates, we shifted from talking about revenue to kilos made. If you're not dealing in dollars daily, then kilos in bags and these metrics are more relevant to the audience.

We have a monthly business update so that everyone who works at Brookfarm understands the greater impact of the job they do whether it's revenue, staff retention or kilos produced. I think it's important to see everyone within each area of the business; I make sure I walk through the business myself so

I can keep my finger on the pulse of the business by having conversations.

On Fridays, we do our weekly wins where everyone gets together and celebrates. We also send an email to everyone so they can focus on what they have achieved and celebrate success. Keeping a cadence is essential.

Purpose

When we connect people to purpose, we inspire them. Purpose is a key driver of employee engagement: 90% of global employees in purpose-driven companies are engaged (Korn Ferry) and purpose-driven employees are 125–225% more productive (Bain & Company).

During the COVID-19 pandemic, people reassessed what was important to them. This isn't a new topic: humans have been searching for meaning and purpose in their personal lives and their careers for some time—seeing as we spend so much time working.

We have discussed the four levels of purpose:

- Organisational purpose.
- Team purpose.
- Meaningful work.
- Personal values.

Thriving leaders communicate and connect people to all four

levels of purpose. (Please go back and read the Purpose section in Chapter 2.)

When people believe their work is meaningful, they are happier. When we have a positive impact on others, the neurotransmitters in our brains release oxytocin, dopamine and serotonin. This is known as the happiness trifecta. How are you helping your team members draw meaning from their work?

Co-create a team purpose that aligns to individuals' personal values. Ensure you connect the work your team members do each day to the organisation's purpose, so they understand why it is important. Your role as a leader is to connect your people to purpose. This means connecting your team to the 'why'.

Start with Why

In Simon Sinek's famous TED Talk, *How Great Leaders Inspire Action*, he says, 'People don't buy what you do, they buy why you do it. When they communicate their purpose or cause first, they communicate in a way that drives decision-making and behaviour. It literally taps the part of the brain that influences behaviour'.

Sinek refers to connecting people to the 'why' by *starting* with 'why'. When we communicate, we should follow his Golden Circle Model by first sharing 'why', then 'how', and then 'what'. Most people share the 'what' and the 'how'.

Think of a key message you need to share. It could be to a key stakeholder, your team or your manager. Then use the Golden Circle to craft your message. In my experience, people often confuse 'why' and 'how' or 'how' and 'what'. Here is an example.

GOLDEN CIRCLE MODEL

WHY?
HOW?
WHAT?

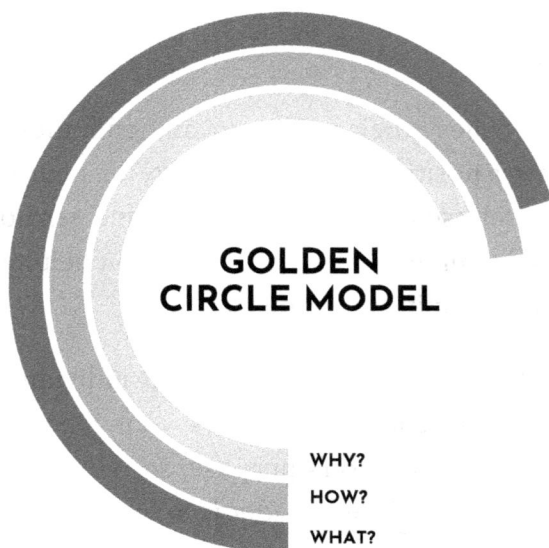

Why: Thriving Culture is a values-based organisation that believes everyone can reach their potential.

How: We empower leaders with the skills and tools to lead a high-performing team.

What: Thriving Culture provides training and coaching to leaders.

Will shares the Brookfarm why.

The purpose was to create the best tasting food that introduced macadamias into our everyday diet. We started this with toasted, natural and gluten-free muesli. We want to inspire people to be healthier. This doesn't mean just macro and micronutrients, we want people to be healthier in general, to enjoy food, have respect for food and have fun with it. Our purpose is to inspire a healthy world.

We connect people at Brookfarm to our purpose through our values. We always link back to our values.

The whole team was involved in shaping the Brookfarm values, so they are meaningful to us all. We assess our people based on our values. This is as important as our accountabilities and is part of the performance framework. From an accountability point of view, it has made people understand where they sit and they are clear about what is required. It is something that we will always be working on: our why and our values.

Internally we say, 'we make the best fucking muesli in the world'. It makes it powerful; it indicates the passion straight away. This language has had a lot of positive impact on the culture and our values.

We connect our staff to our purpose practically by getting people up to the farm so they can see where it all started. We hold an orientation session for our new starters each month and a reorientation for all team members once a year. At these sessions, I make breakfast with one of our products, such as acai bowls, brownies, smoothies or a breakfast crumble. Sometimes my wife Jess and our kids get involved, and my mum. After breakfast, we share the Brookfarm story of how it started. My mum, Pam, was a dentist, and my dad, Martin, was a film director and producer. We share how we came to purchase this macadamia farm with another family and how we progressed to take over the farm, regenerate rainforests and create the products that we sell today. We do an analysis and taste test of one of our products, then we review it together. If there are good suggestions from the orientation and reorientation, we will make those changes to the product. We also take them on a farm and rainforest tour and visit our three main sites.

Our staff are committed experts in our products. A lot of improvement is staff driven. Mum looks after new product development; she holds monthly workshops focused on quality and improving our products.

In these workshops, we compare against our competitors to make the best possible product: bake time, colour, consistency—we track it all through our quality system. Our staff feel proud, and we want them to know that they make the best possible product.

Storytelling

Since humans first roamed the earth, they have communicated via storytelling. From visual stories on cave walls to spoken stories passed down from generations to writing narratives on paper. It is very human to share stories. The power of storytelling in business has become apparent from leadership, marketing and sales perspectives. Storytelling helps to convey purpose, and gain loyalty and commitment. It sparks emotions, personalises you and helps people remember key messages. Storytelling helps to build your credibility. It gets people's attention in the overly saturated communication environment we live in.

We like to think that we are logical creatures, but in reality, we are driven by emotions. So what's the science behind storytelling? Chemicals in the brain like cortisol (assists in formulating memories), oxytocin (empathy and building trust) and dopamine (regulates our emotions) are released when we hear a story. Our brains interpret stories and form meaning by connecting to our own ideas and experiences.

In her book *Ignite,* Gabrielle Dolan shares that when storytelling, we need to make it personal, use humour wisely, use emotion over data, start smart and end smart. Your story should demonstrate your credibility and passion. Data, facts and figures can be boring and disengaging. Couple these with an interesting story and people are more likely to remember the story that supported the data. Draw the insight and humanise it in a way that is relatable.

All good stories have characters, a beginning, middle and end, and a key message. You need to create a narrative that paints a picture of your message. When sharing a story, be authentic and show some vulnerability. Decide what emotion you want to elicit: is it a funny story, a sad story or an inspiring story?

Will encourages storytelling at Brookfarm.

Brookfarm is different because we started as macadamia farmers, and through that farming process, we saw how beneficial it was to be more in sync with the natural environment. It was better for the business of farming macadamias to regenerate rainforests and use an integrated pest management approach that flowed into the food quality.

Our experience on our macadamia farm completely influenced my parents to create Brookfarm.

It is important that our staff are connected to something more than a company making muesli and granola. It's not just a story. It is real life; it is tangible and true. It is important for our staff, customers and consumers to know our story, our plans for the future and that the story will continue long term.

We are rarer than we think. Most people don't make products that taste this good. That is a minimum standard we expect of ourselves.

Communication structure

I've been on several communication courses over the years and they all follow a tried-and-tested format:

- Tell them what you are going to say.
- Tell them.
- Tell them what you told them.

This is a standard format for communicating information—repetition is key, remember. The important point is that it needs to be combined with anecdotes that will engage and trigger the emotional part of the brain. This makes the experience more engaging. You want to elicit an emotional reaction, whether it be laughter, passion, sadness, anger or hope—you want them to feel something.

A compelling hook

The first minute is the most important. People are easily distracted, so you need to land and have a hook in the first minute to draw the audience in. Consider these ideas for making your introduction engaging:

- A thought-provoking story.
- An attention-grabbing statistic.
- A remarkable fact.
- A metaphor or analogy.
- Rhetorical questions.
- An audacious statement.
- Show a powerful or meaningful image.

In Amy Cuddy's TED Talk, she begins with, 'So I want to start by offering you a free no-tech life hack, and all it requires of you is this: that you change your posture for two minutes'. This is an example of an audacious statement. She asks the audience to do an audit of their bodies and uses powerful images and videos coupled with humour—all in the first minute.

Simon Sinek starts his TED Talk with three questions: 'How do you explain when things don't go as we assume? Or better, how do you explain when others are able to achieve things that seem to defy all of the assumptions? For example: Why is Apple so innovative?' He has hooked you in with some key rhetorical questions.

Outline

Outline the agenda and the tagline of the key messages you will share and communicate the journey you will take the audience on, so they know what is coming. This is where repetition begins.

Key messages

The rule of three is a principle for writing or speaking. Information presented in threes is more memorable and effective. This is why the communication structure has three key messages.

For each key message, state the point clearly in a punchy sentence. Then substantiate this statement with remarkable facts, relevant examples, thought-provoking stories, attention-grabbing statistics, and memorable metaphors and analogies that emphasise your message. You don't need to include all of these—maybe one or two for each key message. Conclude the key message with the point stated as a tagline in five words or less. Now, move to your next key message.

Recap

This is the mini conclusion. Explain what you have said to bring the message together. What is the call to action or key takeaway for the audience? What do you want them to think, feel or do?

Strong close

This is your drop-the-mic moment. You want a closing statement that links back to your compelling hook. Make it something that leaves your audience thinking or wanting more.

To close out her TED Talk, Amy Cuddy says, 'They need their bodies, privacy and two minutes, and it can significantly change the outcomes of their life'. She links back to the audacious statement in her hook.

And Simon Sinek closes with, 'And it's those who start with "why" that have the ability to inspire those around them or find others who inspire them'. This is a strong close that inspires and anchors the whole talk.

Here is a simple model for remembering how to structure your communication by storytelling.

Communicating change

Change is normal. We are constantly evolving, improving and adapting the way we do things. Thriving leaders need to lead and

01 Compelling hook

Something memorable. What's in it for them?

02 Outline

Frame what you will discuss.

03 Key message 1

- State your message
- Support it with facts, examples, statistics, stories or metaphors
- The 'so what' for the audience – key point/tag line in <5 words

04 Key message 2

- State your message
- Support it with facts, examples, statistics, stories or metaphors
- The 'so what' for the audience – key point/tag line in <5 words

05 Key message 3

- State your message
- Support it with facts, examples, statistics, stories or metaphors
- The 'so what' for the audience – key point/tag line in <5 words

06 Recap

- Mini conclusion
- Call to action – what do you want the audience to think, feel or do?

07 Memorable close

Close by linking back to the hook.

communicate change effectively. This creates certainty even when we live in an ambiguous world. Leaders and the people they lead often experience change simultaneously.

Understanding change

The Kubler Ross Change Curve describes the four stages people go through when dealing with change. They are denial, anger, acceptance and commitment. This is one of the most popular models to explain change and it originated from a model that helped people understand the grief felt by the terminally ill. It was soon realised that the four stages applied to all change—including organisational change.

People experience change differently and will move through the change curve at different rates. When a team member is in the denial stage, they are likely to be in shock from the change. This is a time to clearly communicate bite-sized, relevant information. Too much information can cause overwhelm. The second stage is anger. Anger is driven by fear of the change and emotions take over. This is where team members will resist the change. Thriving leaders try to accelerate this phase by actively listening and offering support.

Once people reach acceptance, they have stopped focusing on what was lost. When they move to commitment, they are completely on board with the change and are experiencing the benefits. Leaders must ensure they celebrate success and communicate stories of what has been achieved.

Leaders need to move through the change curve quickly, so they can lead their team members effectively depending on what stage of the change curve they are experiencing.

Our mindset transition

Bridge's Model of Transition suggests that people fear the transition of change more than the change itself. Change is the external event that happens to someone, whereas transition is the internal, mental process that people go through (what it was to what it will be in the future).

Leaders need to address this psychological transition. Acknowledge that transition starts with an end, loss or letting go. Listen, be empathetic and communicate openly in this stage. Next, people move to a neutral zone, an in-between time when the old is gone but the new isn't here. This is a mental transformation. They often feel confused, uncertain and in a state of flux.

Be clear on the goal, where you are heading and determine opportunities for quick wins. This is where new beginnings start. New understandings, values and attitudes are required to create a new identity. There is a renewed sense of commitment from the team; it is where connecting personal values to the goals and values of the organisation is key. Reward and recognise your team for the transition and change they have been through. Thriving leaders are aware and empathetic, deploy the tactics above and always ensure they communicate with clarity.

How can you help lead your team through transition?

Living in a VUCA environment

We live in a world of uncertainty—a VUCA environment (volatile, uncertain, complex, ambiguous). This term was created by the US military after 'September 11' to explain the international security environment. We now understand that we live in a constantly unpredictable VUCA environment in business. We need to be aware that this environment is destabilising and overwhelming. Leaders must combat a VUCA environment with vision (be future oriented), understanding (through clear communication), clarity (share what you know to build and maintain trust) and agility (respond to changes).

Hearts and minds

Humans make emotional decisions. We need to see value in a change to alter our mindset. When leading change, we need to influence our people to get on board. The Influence Model (*The Four Building Blocks of Change*, 2016) explains that to win the hearts and minds of your team when you are implementing a change, you need a compelling story, reinforcing mechanisms (structures, systems and processes), a skilled team that is ready for the change and a leader (that's you) to role model the desired behaviour. When all these levers are pulled, team members are more likely to alter their mindsets and take on the change. Consider at what points you can bring them into the change—the earlier and more involved they are in the process, the quicker they will buy in. Team members often have the best ideas and insights to enable an ideal change outcome.

Communicate change effectively

Thriving leaders communicate change effectively. Be thoughtful about what information you share with your team. Leaders are often privy to a lot of information, some of which may not be shared at certain times due to its sensitive nature.

Here are some key areas to focus on when communicating change:

- Create a compelling story. Ensure it starts with the 'why' to rally the team around the vision.
- Repetition is key. Often, leaders believe that because they sent an email, people have understood the communication. If it is an important message, it needs to be communicated in multiple ways. Check in with team members to ensure it is understood.
- Have a communication strategy that is multimodal and multi-channelled. This may involve managers at different levels in the organisation reinforcing key messages and listening to team members' concerns.
- Consult with your teams early so they can share their views and feedback.
- Prepare responses to sticky questions so that you don't fumble your way through the response. It is okay to say you don't have the answer to that right now.
- Identify change champions within your organisation. These are advocates who can promote the change and who can communicate, influence and listen to people's concerns.

Will talks about how he communicates change.

We try to be as quick and transparent with communication as possible. Through COVID, we lost cafes and airlines overnight— we were in troubled waters. I immediately put that down on paper: what the future held, security and lack of security, and talked about it with everyone. The feedback was fantastic. People got a lot from it as they were engaged through the process.

> Change management is around commitment and having an open debate. It is essential to give people the opportunity to express their opinions, thoughts and variations about what is happening. Some people need a push as they are not used to speaking up in a public forum. Ask them if they really think something is a good idea. Then get commitment. This way, we move forward with a plan and with clear overt vocalised commitment to the rest of the team. We have used this approach for a number of things, and it has been effective—it creates clarity. It's the difference between consensus and commitment.
>
> Change management means making sure there is a single clear level of accountability for whatever change is being implemented. It is someone's job and they are accountable for it.

Summary

Ensure your communications are clear and simple. Only communicate relevant information to mitigate the risk of overloading staff with too much information.

Use your authentic voice, make it personal and tell stories. People remember stories rather than facts and figures, so anchor your message around a personal story or anecdote.

Being transparent in your communications will build trust. If you don't know the answer to something, let them know that you will get back to them with more information when it is at hand.

Demonstrate conviction, gravitas and presence to appear confident and credible to your audience.

📝 Actions

- Practise using the Golden Circle to communicate key messages and connect your team to the purpose.
- Craft your next communication using the Communication Structure. Use the QR code below for a template.
- Self-reflection:
  - How do you currently communicate?
  - What do you do that is effective?
  - What could you improve?
- Discover your body language and tone of voice:
  - Record yourself presenting.
  - Watch your recording without sound to examine your body language.
  - Watch it with the sound on and listen to your tone of voice and how you say things.
  - Count the number of filler words (umm, so).
- Create a compelling story to communicate your next change.

https://www.thrivingculture.com.au/tlbook

Where to from here?

First, thank you for reading my book. It's now time to apply your learnings to your authentic leadership style. This doesn't happen overnight.

After delivering a ten-month leadership program, participant Mason Taylor, CEO at Superfeast, said, '... it was a content-rich course and I'm likely to have two years of implementation coming to me. The best thing was realising, "Okay this is my job now, my job is to look for opportunities in every issue in my organisation"'.

Embedding these leadership practices takes time. You may also require additional support to learn the skills to lead confidently.

Contact Thriving Culture to participate in:

- A tailored leadership development program for your organisation.
- An eight-week virtual Thriving Leaders Program.
- A Thriving Teams session to build a high-performing team.

At Thriving Culture, I also offer:

- Leadership, Executive and Team Coaching.
- Speaking at your next conference or event.

I'd love to stay connected and hear your thoughts about the book. Feel free to get in touch via any of the following:

Email: claire.gray@thrivingculture.com.au

Website: www.thrivingculture.com.au

LinkedIn: www.linkedin.com/in/leadership-coach-facilitator

Instagram: @thriving.culture

Thanks,

Claire

References

A Trojan Horse? The Implications Of Managerial Coaching For Leadership Theory. (n.d.). Taylor & Francis. https://www.tandfonline.com/doi/abs/10.1080/13678868.2013.771868

Ackerman, C. E., MA. (2022, August 6). *What is Positive Psychology & Why is It Important?* PositivePsychology.com. https://positivepsychology.com/what-is-positive-psychology-definition/#:%7E:text=%E2%80%9CPositive%20psychology%20is%20the%20scientific%20study%20of%20human%20strengths%20and,%2C%20and%20the%20meaningful%20life.%E2%80%9D

Ambady, N., LaPlante, D., Nguyen, T., Rosenthal, R., Chaumeton, N., & Levinson, W. (2001). *Surgeons' Tone of Voice: A Clue to Malpractice History*. Surgery. https://www.surgjournal.com/article/S0039-6060(02)00022-3/pdf

The Authenticity Paradox. (2022, April 15). Harvard Business Review. https://hbr.org/2015/01/the-authenticity-paradox

Basford, T., & Schaninger, B. (2021, March 1). *The Four Building Blocks Of Change*. McKinsey & Company. https://www.mckinsey.com/business-functions/people-and-organizational-performance/our-insights/the-four-building-blocks--of-change

Belyh, A. (2022, January 20). *Understanding the Kubler-Ross Change Curve*. Cleverism. https://www.cleverism.com/understanding-kubler-ross-change-curve/

Bridges Transition Model. (2020, March 12). William Bridges Associates. https://wmbridges.com/about/what-is-transition/

Brown, B. (2015, April 7). *Daring Greatly: How the Courage to Be Vulnerable Transforms the Way We Live, Love, Parent, and Lead* (Reprint). Avery.

Brown, B. (2022, March 1). *The Gifts of Imperfection: 10th Anniversary Edition: Features a new foreword and brand-new tools* (Anniversary). Hazelden Publishing.

Building Strong Coaching Cultures for the Future. (n.d.). Human Capital Institute. https://www.hci.org/research/building-strong-coaching-cultures-future

Clifton, D. O., & Harter, J. K. (n.d.). *Investing in Strengths.* Gallup. https://media.gallup.com/documents/whitepaper--investinginstrengths.pdf

Clutterbuck, D. (n.d.). *The Liberated Coach.* David Clutterbuck Partnership. https://www.davidclutterbuckpartnership.com/wp-content/uploads/The-Liberated-Coach.pdf

Clutterbuck, D. (2007, March 1). *Coaching the Team at Work* (1st ed.). Nicholas Brealey Publishing.

Conley, R. (2018, October 8). *The 5 Causes of Psychological Safety and Why You Need to be a Safe Leader.*

Leading With Trust. https://leadingwithtrust.com/2018/10/08/5-causes-of-psychological-safety/

The Cost Of Poor Leadership On Your Revenue And Culture - Blog -. (n.d.). https://www.gbscorporate.com/blog/the-cost-of-poor-leadership-on-your-revenue-and-culture#:%7E:text=DDI%2C%20a%20leading%20 researcher%20in,%2C%20turnover%2C%20and%20staff%20 dissension

Covey, S. R. (2004). *The 7 Habits of Highly Effective People: Restoring the Character Ethic*. Simon & Schuster.

Cuddy, A. (2012, October 1). *Your Body Language May Shape Who You Are*. TED Talks https://www.ted.com/talks/amy_cuddy_your_body_language_may_shape_who_you_are

The Discipline of Teams. (2015, August 6). Harvard Business Review. https://hbr.org/1993/03/the-discipline-of-teams-2

Discovery Of 'Thought Worms' Opens Window To The Mind. (2020, July 14). Queen's Gazette | Queen's University. https://www.queensu.ca/gazette/stories/discovery-thought-worms-opens-window-mind

Doerr, J., & Page, L. (2018, April 24). *Measure What Matters: How Google, Bono, and the Gates Foundation Rock the World with OKRs* (Illustrated). Portfolio.

Dolan, G. (2015, June 30). *Ignite: Real Leadership, Real Talk, Real Results*. Wiley.

Dweck, C. S. (2007, December 26). *Mindset: The New Psychology of Success* (Updated Edition). Ballantine Books.

Ebbinghaus's Forgetting Curve: Why We Keep Forgetting and What We Can Do About It. (n.d.). Mind Tools. https://www.mindtools.com/pages/article/forgetting-curve.htm#:%7E:text=The%20Forgetting%20Curve%2C%20or%20the,action%20to%20keep%20it%20there.

Engaging Your Employees Is Good, But Don't Stop There. (2017, October 25). Harvard Business Review. https://hbr.org/2015/12/engaging-your-employees-is-good-but-dont-stop-there

Flynn, F. J., & Lide, C. R. (2022, July 25). Communication Miscalibration: The Price Leaders Pay for Not Sharing Enough. *Academy of Management Journal.* https://doi.org/10.5465/amj.2021.0245

Folkman, J., & Zenger, J. (2017, May 2). *Why do so many managers avoid giving praise?* Harvard Business Review. https://hbr.org/2017/05/why-do-so-many-managers-avoid-giving-praise

Gallup, Inc. (2021, May 3). *Employees Who Use Their Strengths Outperform Those Who Don't.* Gallup.com. https://www.gallup.com/workplace/236561/employees-strengths-outperform-don.aspx

Gallup, Inc. (2022a, August 3). *CliftonStrengths Online Talent Assessment | EN - Gallup.* Gallup.com. https://www.gallup.com/cliftonstrengths/en/252137/home.aspx?utm_source=google&utm_medium=cpc&utm_campaign=australia_cs_ecom&utm_term=cliftonstrengths&gclid=Cj0KCQjwpe-aYBhDXARIsAEzItbHIekLsJbnj4t7RWxolOHpzF_pxVstCC-NhbQbhXQdOG0X7XILDIavwaAuBREALw_wcB

Gallup, Inc. (2022b, August 5). *State of the Global Workplace Report - Gallup.* Gallup.com. https://www.gallup.com/workplace/349484/state-of-the-global-workplace-2022-report.aspx

Gallup, Inc. (2022c, August 23). *How to Improve Employee Engagement in the Workplace - Gallup.* Gallup.com. https://www.gallup.com/workplace/285674/improve-employee-engagement-workplace.aspx

Gardner, R. (2022, March 11). *A Complete Guide to the Skill Will Matrix.* AIHR. https://www.aihr.com/blog/skill-will-matrix/

Gatien, V. (2022, January 17). *Employee Pulse Survey Tool.* Officevibe. https://officevibe.com/pulse-survey-tool

GBS Corporate Training. (2017, July 13). *The Cost Of Poor Leadership On Your Revenue And Culture.* https://www.gbscorporate.com/blog/the-cost-of-poor-leadership-on-your-revenue-and-culture

George, B. (2004, July 28). *Authentic Leadership: Rediscovering the Secrets to Creating Lasting Value* (1st ed.). Jossey-Bass.

Glaab, S. (2022, January 14). *Your Strengths' Shadow Side: When They Fail To Support You.* Forbes. https://www.forbes.com/sites/forbescoachescouncil/2022/01/14/your-strengths-shadow-side-when-they-fail-to-support-you/?sh=10c78ddc6dae

Glaser, J. (2013, October 1). *Conversational Intelligence: How Great Leaders Build Trust and Get Extraordinary Results* (1st ed.). Routledge.

Goleman, D. (2005, September 27). *Emotional Intelligence: Why It Can Matter More Than IQ* (10th Anniversary). Random House Publishing Group.

Goleman, D. (2009, July 20). *Working with Emotional Intelligence.* Bloomsbury Publishing.

Google. (n.d.). *Understand Team Effectiveness.* Re:Work. https://rework.withgoogle.com/print/guides/5721312655835136/

Grant, A. (2021, February 2). *Think Again: The Power of Knowing What You Don't Know.* Viking.

Gregory, L. (2016, June 22). *Difficult Conversations: How To Discuss What Matters Most in Communication. Coping With Difficult People and Moments in Life.* CreateSpace Independent Publishing Platform.

Grossman, D. (2018, April 10). *The Cost of Poor Communication*. SHRM. https://www.shrm.org/resourcesandtools/hr-topics/organizational-and-employee-development/pages/the-cost-of-poor-communication.aspx#:%7E:text=David%20Grossman%20reported%20in%20%E2%80%9CThe,communication%20to%20and%20between%20employees.

Gyllensten, K., & Palmer, S. (2014). *Increased Employee Confidence: A Benefit of Coaching*. APA PsycNet. https://psycnet.apa.org/record/2014-28285-006

Hawkins, P. (2021, June 29). *Leadership Team Coaching: Developing Collective Transformational Leadership* (4th ed.). Kogan Page.

Head, Heart and Guts: How the World's Best Companies Develop Complete Leaders. (2010, March 18). Jossey-Bass.

High-Performing Teams Need Psychological Safety: Here's How to Create It. (2022, August 10). Harvard Business Review. https://hbr.org/2017/08/high-performing-teams-need-psychological-safety-heres-how-to-create-it

How to Keep A Players Productive. (2020, October 24). Harvard Business Review. https://hbr.org/2006/09/how-to-keep-a-players-productive

ICF, the Gold Standard in Coaching | Read About ICF. (2022, August 18). International Coaching Federation. https://coachingfederation.org/about#:%7E:text=What%20is%20Coaching%3F,of%20imagination%2C%20productivity%20and%20leadership.

Kubler-Ross, E. (2022, September 12). *On Death And Dying - What The Dying Have To Teach Doctors, Nurses, Clergy And Their Own Families* (Later prt.). Macmillan.

Landsberg, M. (2015). *The Tao of Coaching: Boost Your Effectiveness at Work by Inspiring and Developing Those Around You.* Adfo Books.

Lencioni, P. (2012, March 19). *The Five Dysfunctions of a Team.* John Wiley & Sons Inc (US).

Leonard, J. (2020, September 30). *How to handle impostor syndrome.* https://www.medicalnewstoday.com/articles/321730

Maslow, A. H., GP Editors, & General Press. (2022, June 1). *A Theory of Human Motivation (Hardcover Library Edition)* (1st ed.). General Press.

Microsoft. (2022, March 16). *Great Expectations: Making Hybrid Work Work.* https://www.microsoft.com/en-us/worklab/work-trend-index/great-expectations-making-hybrid-work-work

O'Neill, E. (2021, November 11). *In Conversation with Dr Alex Linley – Tapping into Strengths.* Langley Group. https://langleygroup.com.au/in-conversation-with-dr-alex-linley-tapping-into-strengths/

Patterson, K., Grenny, J., McMillan, R., Switzler, A., & Maxfield, D. (2013, June 14). *Crucial Accountability: Tools for Resolving Violated Expectations, Broken Commitments, and Bad Behavior, Second Edition (Paperback)* (2nd ed.). McGraw Hill.

The Practical Art of Persuasion. (2014, July 23). Harvard Business Review. https://hbr.org/2011/03/the-practical-art-of-persuasio

The Practice of Adaptive Leadership: Tools and Tactics for Changing Your Organization and the World by Ronald Heifetz, Alexander Grashow, and Marty Linsky. (2010, March). *Personnel Psychology, 63*(1), 255–258. https://doi.org/10.1111/j.1744-6570.2009.01168_4.x

Reina, D. S., & Reina, M. L. (2000, February). Trust and Betrayal in the Workplace. *Advances in Developing Human Resources, 2*(1), 121–121. https://doi.org/10.1177/152342230000200112

Schneider, M. (2021, January 5). *A Google Study Revealed That the Best Managers Use Emotional Intelligence And Share This 1 Trait.* Inc.com. https://www.inc.com/michael-schneider/a-google-study-revealed-that-best-managers-use-emotional-intelligence-share-this-1-trait.html

Scott, K. M. (n.d.). *Radical Candor: How to Get What You Want by Saying What You mean (Expert Thinking).*

Seligman, M., & Csikszentmihalyi, M. (2000). *Positive Psychology. An Introduction.* NIH. https://pubmed.ncbi.nlm.nih.gov/11392865/

Sinek, S. (2010, May 4). *How Great Leaders Inspire Action.* TED Talks. https://www.ted.com/talks/simon_sinek_how_great_leaders_inspire_action?language=en

Stanier, B. M. (2016, February 29). *The Coaching Habit: Say Less, Ask More & Change the Way You Lead Forever* (1st ed.). Page Two.

Stone, D., & Heen, S. (2015, March 31). *Thanks for the Feedback: The Science and Art of Receiving Feedback Well* (Reprint). Penguin Books.

The Economist Intelligence Unit. (n.d.). *Communication Barriers in the Modern Workplace.* https://d2slcw3kip6qmk.

cloudfront.net/marketing/pages/chart/ebooks/FINAL_ EIU_Lucidchart_March2018.pdf

The Predictive Index. (2021, September 21). *Annual CEO Benchmarking Report 2021*. https://www.predictiveindex. com/ceo-benchmarking-report-2021/

Trimboli, O. (2019a). *Deep Listening: Impact Beyond Words*. Oscar Trimboli.

The Value of Belonging at Work: The Business Case for Investing in Workplace Inclusion. (n.d.). https://grow.betterup.com/ resources/the-value-of-belonging-at-work-the-business-case-for-investing-in-workplace-inclusion-event

VIA Character Strengths Survey & Character Reports. (n.d.). VIA Institute. https://www.viacharacter.org/

Why Do So Many Managers Avoid Giving Praise? (2021, August 30). Harvard Business Review. https://hbr.org/2017/05/ why-do-so-many-managers-avoid-giving-praise

Wightman, E. (2022, April 19). *2022 HR Industry Benchmark Report*. ELMO Software AU. https://elmosoftware.com.au/ resources/research-reports/2022-hr-industry-benchmark-report/

Williams, B. T. (2022, January 14). *The Boss Factor: Workers Quit Bosses, Not Companies*. ExecEd Navigator. https://execed. economist.com/blog/industry-trends/boss-factor-workers-quit-bosses-not-companies

Zenger, J. (2012, August 7). *We Wait Too Long to Train Our Leaders*. Harvard Business Review. https://hbr.org/2012/12/ why-do-we-wait-so-long-to-trai

www.ingramcontent.com/pod-product-compliance
Lightning Source LLC
Chambersburg PA
CBHW071554210326
41597CB00019B/3238